To Kim,
Blessings,
Rosemary Ellen Guiley

Dream Messages from the Afterlife

Dream Messages from the Afterlife

Rosemary Ellen Guiley

Visionary Living, Inc.
New Milford, Connecticut
Copyright 2013

Dream Messages from the Afterlife

By Rosemary Ellen Guiley

Cover design by Raúl daSilva
with the illustration rendered by Ray daSilva
inspired by the art of Raphael Lacoste

ISBN: 978-0-9857243-5-1 (pbk)

Visionary Living, Inc.
New Milford, Connecticut
www.visionaryliving.com

Contents

Introduction

One of the most significant dreams I have ever had in my entire life was a meeting with my father about two weeks after he died. The environment was both familiar and surreal, and we both acknowledged the fact that Dad was no longer living. The meeting, and the dream itself, were not wish fulfillment or imagination. To this day, I know that I had a genuine meeting with my dead father. It was not anything I summoned, yet it came from and was driven by a higher purpose that was meaningful to us both.

In the course of life, a person is likely to have a number of dreams that are so vivid and powerful that the details of them are never forgotten, unlike most dreams that happen during sleep. At least one of those memorable dreams is likely to be a meeting with the dead, or contain a significant message from the dead, or be a glimpse of the afterlife. These dreams can alleviate grief, change our views on dying, death and the afterlife, and bring peace and healing.

Afterlife dreams are most likely to happen after the death of a loved one. They can also occur during times of stress and trauma, and during serious illness.

These dreams are real experiences that take place in another reality. In this reality, we are able to transcend limitations of the physical world. Our dreams are teaching tools, showing us how to grow and improve, even in the depths of our sorrow and longing for those who have passed on. Dreams are the original language of the spiritual path.

The ancients understood how dreams connect us to the spiritual realms, and deep in our hearts we still know it today. Dreams are a straight connection to the divine heart of the cosmos. In dreams, we can have contact with the dead, receive high spiritual guidance, meet otherworldly beings, visit other dimensions, and explore new frontiers of consciousness.

Even before the dream with my father, I was intensely interested in dreams, especially their spiritual content. From my early teens, I kept a dream journal that, over time, revealed a great deal of insight into myself, and also chronicled my journeys into other realms. I became convinced at any early age that dreams are one of our most important allies in making our way through life—and beyond.

Many people who have a profound afterlife dream have not paid significant attention to their dreams, and they wonder how to interpret this "big one." Was it real? Was it imagination? Are dreams reliable? The dream holds something quite precious. If they risk sharing it, will it be explained away? If someone, especially an authority figure such as a counselor or therapist, declares the dream to be "just" grief and wish fulfillment, that precious truth is diminished, perhaps even lost.

This book is an exploration of afterlife dreaming, experiences shared by human beings throughout history that attest to the survival of the soul, and to our continuing bond with loved ones.

Montague Ullman, who was a psychiatrist, psychoanalyst and parapsychologist who co-founded the Dream Laboratory at the Maimonides Medical Center in Brooklyn, said that dreams are vital to the survival of humanity as a whole. In addition to having personal significance, dreams have a collective importance.

We share the same dreams with others, but more important, we all share the dream landscape in terms of other realities. We have an ancient and enduring legacy of dream contact with the dead and the divine. The experiences we have today are similar to ones had by our distant ancestors. We are participating in an eternal web of life, death, the afterlife and rebirth. Our dreams reveal the majesty of this cycle. By acknowledging and sharing our dreams, we continue that heritage.

—Rosemary Ellen Guiley

1

Dream Messages from the Dead

Just two weeks after his 49th birthday, Bob suffered a heart attack at four AM one morning and died. His death, completely unexpected, was a severe shock to his wife, Anne. Soon after Bob's passing, Anne had the most profound dream she had ever experienced:

> We were holding each other and I felt something running down my leg. I looked and it was blood. Bob tried to help me wipe it away and I realized I had no skin at all. I was just raw meat. He tried to gently stroke me to help me stop bleeding. I knew that he was trying to tell me he was there for me, and although I felt totally raw, exposed and unprepared for his death, that he would help me.

The dream graphically expressed the intensity of Anne's grief: total rawness and exposure, and a bleeding away of vitality. Years later, she still experienced waves of emotion just recounting the dream. Yet despite its painful imagery, the dream contained a healing balm as well:

1

To have my lover gently stroking my raw body to help soothe me, in retrospect, was a message about the work I was about to begin toward my spiritual rebirth. His death freed me from physical concerns, and the knowledge that we don't die has changed my life. Who needs skin to connect? We don't!

Bob's death led Anne on a spiritual journey in which she awakened her natural gifts of intuition, psychic ability, and healing. The comfort she felt in the dream gave her the courage and energy to undertake the journey.

Dream meetings with people who have died are seldom sad, but bring comfort, relief, and joy instead. They have a transformative, healing power that is felt on both sides of the veil. Many dreams of the dead are so intense and realistic that people often wonder if they had a dream or a "real experience."

Dreams of the dead are often symbolic and are a natural part of the mourning process. In grief counseling, they might be treated as wish fulfillments and emotional releases, such as for the last conversation we never had, or the ways we miss someone. The dead also appear as ordinary dream symbols, representing something about the dreamer or waking life. For example, a deceased father in a dream might represent an authority figure.

Many other dreams of the dead are distinctly different. They are true encounters with the dead in an alternate reality, the dreamscape. Dreams take us beyond the limits of the physical world during sleep. Under certain circumstances, we have reunions with the dead. These special dreams are purposeful, to impart important information, and heal wounds and grief.

Hugging Dad

After Valerie lost her father, she missed him greatly and wanted once to hug him. One night she cried herself to sleep thinking about hugging Dad. In Dianne Arcangel's *Afterlife Encounters*, she relates what happened:

After finally falling asleep, I had the most vivid dream I have ever had.

I was a little girl again, we were in the same house I grew up in, and Dad appeared exactly as he did back then—young, handsome, and well-dressed. I will always remember my encounters with him in that dream.

In my first encounter I said, "Daddy, you're here! You really are here!" With that, I ran up to him like a child does with a parent, and I literally clenched my arms around his waist and would not let go. He just smiled at me.

Valerie then "awoke" in her dream and saw her father standing in front of the closet. He was quietly taking off his tie, as though he did not want to wake her. He told her to go back to sleep.

She got out of bed, and saw him walking down the hallway.

... I jumped in front of him and said, "Daddy, Daddy, you're really still here." I still couldn't believe he was there. I grabbed him again around his waist and held on for dear life. I could feel him hugging me. Neither of us would let go.

I will never forget the physical intensity of that hug. Today I believe he came to give me what I so desperately called out for—a hug. I got what I asked for and so much more. I realize it wasn't just a dream—spirits often visit us in dreams because it's the easiest way to communicate.

After-death contact happens to many people who have lost loved ones, and is more likely to happen in dreams than in waking visions and impressions. The afterlife dreams we have today have a long history of similar experiences shared by our distant ancestors, and with other people all around the world. Relationships, especially within the family, are seen as continuing after death, and the ancestral spirits have the ability to interact in the lives of the living. Dream contact with the dead has a beneficial effect for both the living and the dead.

Types of afterlife dreams

Perhaps you have had a significant dream involving contact or communication with the dead, or a vision of the afterlife. Most after life dreams occur in several types:

Farewells

Farewell dreams often involve people who are terminally ill. The dreamer dreams that the ill person comes to them to say good-bye as they leave the earth plane. Sometimes the farewell is within an intense, lucid dream. Other times, the person awakens—or thinks they awaken—and sees the departing person standing at the foot of the bed, or beside the bed. Their image is vivid and then fades away. The next day, the dreamer discovers that the person died the night before, or in the early morning hours.

Farewell encounter dreams also happen in cases of sudden and unexpected death, such as through accidents or violent ends. The dying person appears at a moment of extreme crisis or imminent death. In psychical research, these dreams are called "crisis apparitions." They usually appear to a loved one or friend with whom the dying person has close emotional ties. Sometimes their appearance reveals the manner of their death. Their clothing may look burned if they died in a fire, for example, or the figures may gesture to show their fatal wounds.

Reassurances

In reassurance dreams, a dead person imparts the message that everything is all right. It is not unusual for the dead person to appear restored in health and youth, and be radiant with happiness and energy. Reassurance dreams usually happen within a few days or weeks of a person's passing, when worry and grief are at a peak with the living—but they can also occur months or even years after someone has died.

Life guidance

A dead person, not necessarily recently deceased, appears in a dream to impart advice, warnings, solutions to problems and creative ideas, or to bestow blessings of love and forgiveness. Their messages may be brief and couched in dream symbolism. Sometimes they are able to have a long conversation with the dreamer. The meeting is realistic and may even involve touching and hugging. Sometimes the dreamer will not remember all the conversational details upon awakening, but will nonetheless "know" what is to be done.

Unfinished business

Few people are able to die with full closure of every detail in their lives. Most of those concerns fall away with the transition to the afterlife. In some cases, however, there are important matters to be addressed, and the dead find a way to get their concerns through to the living. Such concerns usually involve their estates, burial requests, last wishes, and so on.

Helping the dead

Our religions and spiritual faiths teach us that one of the best ways we can help the dead is through prayer, which sends tremendous spiritual energy between realms. On occasion, the dead need some extra help, and may appear in dreams to reach out. If they died suddenly, they may be confused about where they are. In lucid dreams, a conversation can take place. Sometimes the dreamer awakens knowing they must pray for the dead.

In addition, there are other types of dreams involving the afterlife:

Dreams that foretell death

Precognitive dreams warning of impending death have been documented since ancient times. People dream of the deaths of others and, rarely, of their own passing. The dead are often the messengers.

Dreams of the dying and deathbed visions

Dreams and dream-like visions of the afterlife occur to individuals who are nearing death. Terminally ill patients may begin experiencing vivid contact with the dead and previews of the afterlife up to several weeks before they pass. Sometimes caregivers and family and friends participate in the experiences as well, by sharing visions and having their own corroborating dreams.

Previews of the afterlife

Dreams take us to the edge of the afterlife, to places of transition and glimpses of what lies beyond. We have meetings with the dead, and spiritual guides and helpers who explain the afterlife to us. These extraordinary dreams occur throughout life, often as part of spiritual awakenings and major transitions in life.

Characteristics of afterlife dreams

Dream encounters with the dead are so real that we wonder whether or not we were dreaming or somehow awake. Sometimes there is an "awakening" that is part of the dream experience. Here are some of the major traits of afterlife dreams:

Visions and Voices

The dead appear visually in dreams in a variety of forms. They may look as they did when they were alive, and still seem very much alive. They may be wearing the clothing they wore when they died. In some cases, their "bodies" may show the manner of their deaths, such as wounds. In some dreams, the dead are more ghost-like—semi-transparent, or with partial bodies (usually the upper torso). They may speak or convey mental thoughts. Sometimes the figures are silent. In yet other dreams, the dead are not visually present but are sensed by the dreamer.

Unusual light

The dead are often bathed in an unearthly glow or a brilliant white or golden light. Sometimes the entire dream landscape is full of brilliant light. If the dreamer awakens, the bedroom may be infused with light as well, such as in the following descriptions:

> ...the light was so bright I could hardly keep my eyes open...
> ...it was a brilliant light unlike anything I have ever seen, and it had an almost electrical quality to it...

> ...there was a pale golden radiance that lit up the entire room...

> ...My mother was enveloped in this wonderful light. She looked at me and smiled and then she and the light faded away. I just knew in my heart that she had just passed away.

Unusual light is also characteristic of lucidity in dreams, a common trait of dream visits from the dead, as described below.

Lucidity

Dreams of the dead are often lucid, that is, we know we're in the dream while we are having it. Lucid dreams are characterized by brilliant light; a strange atmosphere or setting, such as an electrical charge to the air or a "thick" feel to the air; vivid and unusual colors; and even smells associated with the deceased, such as a favorite perfume. There may also be heightened emotions, and the ability to touch the dead person, who feels alive and solid. Communication is rarely verbal but telepathic, as though words are impressed in the dreamer's mind.

Lucid dreams can be directed and controlled; the extent varies according to the context of the dream and the ability of the dreamer to stay lucid and in control. Sometimes lucidity disappears as soon as the dreamer realizes he is dreaming. Frequent lucid dreamers have a natural skill at directing their dreams, while others can learn it through practice.

Lucid dreams with the dead carry a strong emotional impact for the dreamer, who awakens certain that he or she has actually been with the dead. "It was not a dream—it was real!" they will say.

Lucid dreams, including those that bridge the afterlife, have been recognized since ancient times. In the 4th century BCE, Aristotle mentioned the existence of lucid dreaming. The earliest known written account of a lucid dream in Western history is contained in a letter written in 415 CE by Augustine, who described the lucid dream of a Carthaginian physician, Gennadius. The purpose of the dream was to convince Gennadius of life after death. In the dream, Gennadius is greeted by a young man who demonstrates the existence of the afterlife. Augustine wrote:

> As God would in no wise forsake a man so merciful in his disposition and conduct, there appeared to him [Gennadius] in sleep a youth of remarkable appearance and commanding presence, who said to him: "Follow me."
>
> Following him, he came to a city where he began to hear on the right hand sounds of a melody so exquisitely sweet as to surpass anything he had ever heard. When he inquired what it was, his guide said: "It is the hymn of the blessed and the holy." What he reported himself to have seen on the left hand escapes my remembrance. He awoke; the dream vanished, and he thought of it as only a dream.
>
> On a second night, however, the same youth appeared to Gennadius, and asked whether he recognized him, to which he replied that he knew him well, without the slightest uncertainty. Thereupon he asked Gennadius where he had become acquainted with him. There also his memory failed him not as to the proper reply: He narrated the whole vision, and the hymns of the saints which, under his guidance, he had been taken to hear, with all the readiness natural to recollection of some very recent experience. On this the youth inquired whether it was in sleep or when awake that he had seen what he had just narrated. Gennadius answered:

"In sleep."

The youth then said: "You remember it well; it is true that you saw these things in sleep, but I would have you know that even now you are seeing in sleep."

Hearing this, Gennadius was persuaded of its truth, and in his reply declared that believed it. Then his teacher went on to say: "Where is your body now?"

He answered: "In my bed."

"Do you know," said the youth, "that the eyes in this body of yours are now bound and closed, and at rest, and that with these eyes you are seeing nothing?"

He answered: "I know it."

"What then," said the youth, "are the eyes with which you see me?"

He, unable to discover what to answer to this, was silent. While he hesitated, the youth unfolded to him what he was endeavoring to teach him by these questions, and forthwith said: "As while you are asleep and lying on your bed these eyes of your body are now unemployed and doing nothing, and yet you have eyes with which you behold me, and enjoy this vision, so, after your death, while your bodily eyes shall be wholly inactive, there shall be in you a life by which you shall still live, and a faculty of perception by which you shall still perceive. Beware, therefore, after this of harboring doubts as to whether the life of man shall continue after death." This believer says that by this means all doubts as to this matter were removed from him. By whom was he taught this but by the merciful, providential care of God?

Lucid dreaming is part of "ordinary dreaming," too. More than one-half of the adult population has at least a few spontaneous lucid dreams during life, and nearly one-quarter of the adult population has a spontaneous lucid dream about once a month. Some individuals are frequent lucid dreamers. People who have had near-death experiences (NDEs) also have more lucid dreams than other people. For many people, the occasional or rare lucid dream will involve a meaningful encounter with the dead.

Physicist Fred Alan Wolf has suggested that lucid dreams—and perhaps dreams in general—are visits to parallel universes. Wolf calls the ability to lucid dream "parallel universe awareness."

The Other Side is one of those parallel universes alongside the realm of the living.

Out-of-body experiences

Dream visits with the dead may involve a sensation of leaving the physical body and traveling at great speed. The out-of-body dreaming is done in a second body that duplicates the physical. We may find ourselves visiting distant places on earth, entering the dreamscapes of others, or visiting a between-place where we can have meetings with the dead and spiritual guides.

OBE dreams usually happen spontaneously, though some individuals learn how to induce them. It is not necessary to sleep first, though the sleep state is conducive to the experience.

The second body is called the astral body, the etheric body, the soul body, the second body, or the dreambody. It acts as a nonphysical, subtle vehicle for consciousness. Sometimes dreamers are aware of it and can see it, and other times they are not aware of having any form at all.

In 1958, an American radio and television executive named Robert A. Monroe began traveling spontaneously out-of-body while relaxed and near sleep. Monroe had incredible experiences not limited to the earth plane, but to realms in which he visited the afterlife transition plane, and had contact with discarnate humans and a variety of nonhuman beings.

Monroe's initial experiences began when he would lie down to go to sleep. Before he reached sleep, when he was in the hypnagogic stage, he would experience a buzzing and vibrating, and feel himself lift out of his body. Like an explorer touching the shores of an unknown land, Monroe explored and mapped this state of being. He first experienced what he called Locale I, which involved people and places in the physical world. He could instantly go to distant locations and see what people there were doing.

Then he pushed into Locale II, or the astral plane, where most OBEs and dreams occur. Many of the places that he visited in Locale II had a familiar feel to them. They are the creations of consciousness, he said, and have been mapped and visited by countless souls. Locale II is vast and incorporates our ideas of the afterlife. Here Monroe met the dead as well as nonhuman entities, many of whom were intelligent and could communicate with him. The lower reaches of Locale II are closest to earth, he said, and are populated by unpleasant entities obsessed with emotional and sexual gratification. The higher reaches are pleasant, beautiful places.

Locale III is located on the other side of a hole in the space-time continuum, and appears to be a near-identical physical world to ours—perhaps a parallel universe.

Beyond Locale III are many levels remaining to be explored, some of which are beyond our ability to comprehend, he said.

Dreams or waking visions?

Dream visits with the dead happen during different stages of sleep. Sometimes a person takes a nap and falls into a light reverie called the hypnagogic stage, where the brain shifts from wakefulness into sleep. Awareness of a presence may rouse the sleeper, who perceives the dead in a type of waking vision.

Sometimes it is difficult to know where the border is that divides wakefulness from sleep. The dreamer may think he is awake, but is experiencing a false awakening in a lucid dream. In other cases, the dreamer may be roused from sleep and have a waking vision. In such cases, the dreaming state of consciousness may be significant for the experience to take place. Ultimately, it does not matter in terms of the actual contact with the dead—the experience happens in the most appropriate way for each individual.

Ancient peoples made little or no distinction between dreams and other kinds of visionary experiences that happened during both day and night, in sleep, trance and waking consciousness. The emphasis was on the content of the experience.

To the ancients, the gods and the dead emerged from their own domains to enter the realm of mortals or meet them in a way station. Our dream visits with the dead in modern times reinforce that concept. The dream is able to bridge realms in ways that may be difficult, even impossible, in waking consciousness.

If you have an encounter dream involving a dead person, it is important to trust your feelings and intuition about the dream. People often awaken with a certainty about what the dream means. It is important to consider such factors as mourning and wish fulfillment, but these are not the only explanations for encounter dreams.

The mechanisms of afterlife dreams

Dream visits with the dead operate under conditions and perhaps even "rules" that we do not fully understand. Not everyone who dies makes a return in a dramatic dream. Some make more than one appearance. What's more, the choice of recipient is sometimes puzzling to the living. For example, a spouse or family member may not receive a dream visit, but a casual friend does. The absence of a reassuring dream visit can be quite distressing to the grieving, who may wonder if they are being punished, or the dead choose not to visit them. Some wonder, "Why did I have this dream?" while others wonder, "Why did someone else have a dream that was meant for me?"

The answer to this mystery lies in the unknown reaches of consciousness. Visitation dreams usually occur where strong emotional ties exist, but emotional ties do not guarantee a visit. Likewise, desire to have contact cannot cause a visit to happen. Dream messages and visits from the afterlife seem to occur under a complex set of circumstances. People who have innate psychic ability and who meditate are more likely to have lucid and OBE dreams, but those qualities also do not guarantee a visit from the dead. And, people who have had no marked prior psychic experiences may have intense dream visits.

Despite the variables and unknowns, it is possible to improve the conditions that enhance dream visitations, and those will be discussed later on in this book.

The boundary that divides the world of the living from the afterlife is a powerful one. We do not know the conditions that exist on the Other Side that must be engineered for pathways to open, even in dreams. When the dead visit, they often tell us they have limited time, as though the window of opportunity is narrow.

Another factor is the way a person dreams. All humans may share the dreamscape and the act of dreaming, but there are unique factors for each person that are beyond our present comprehension. Thus, a dream visit is like electricity that finds the path of least resistance. There is an intended visit, a push from the Other Side, and a pull from the side of the living. The dream is attracted to the best channel—which may account for friends receiving visits instead of family members.

The following dream experiences of a middle-aged woman illustrate how this may happen:

I have had two dreams about loved ones who have died. The first was my grandmother. The second was my mother-in-law. Both dreams could be described more as "visits" than dreams. What I mean is both times the women were talking to me more than they were part of a dream sequence. Both times the women were reassuring me and telling me they were with me. Both times I woke up happy and grateful that I had seen them.

Both dreams were very vivid. The second time (after the one with my mother-in-law) I wrote down every detail I could remember—it was about four pages long. What struck me as odd was that I can remember thanking her for visiting me. She just smiled. She wanted me to reassure her son (my husband) that she was with him. I asked her why she didn't just visit him and she replied that she couldn't "because of the way that he dreams."

The dreamer was not certain what her mother-in-law meant by that re-mark, which implied that an obstacle existed that prevented access to her husband's dream states. The wife acknowledged that she was naturally in-tuitive and sensitive to the thoughts and feelings of others. She also had fre-quent precognitive and lucid dreams, which she could control. She enjoyed dreaming because it was "sort of like enjoying a good book or a movie." Consequently, she may have been easier to reach from the Other Side.

She described more characteristics of both dreams:

> The dream with my mother-in-law was very different. I knew I was asleep but did not feel as if I had to try to stay asleep. I remember thinking to myself, as she was walking down the road toward me, "Oh my gosh that's N. I had better not try to control anything. I better just let it happen." (I did not want to wake up and miss talking to her.)
>
> The first thing I said was, "Thank you for visiting me. I miss you so much."
>
> She smiled as if she understood. We both knew I was dreaming. The strongest, clearest things were: the feel of her hands in mine (smooth and plump); the feel of her cheek against mine when I hugged her; smell; her clothes (she dressed as she had every day); her thoughts to me were very clear (she wanted me to tell my husband that everything would be alright, she was with him); her little dog. I did not hear her speak but rather it seemed her responses were thoughts that I could hear.
>
> When I dreamed about my grandmother, it felt like the current time but, I was small. She was holding me on her lap. The dream with my mother-in-law was definitely in real time. My daughter was with me. She was her current age (nine). As a matter a fact when I said to my mother-in-law, "This is K.," she smiled and said, "I know." In a way that made me feel as if she had been watching the whole time (she died when K. was 18

months old).

One thing did surprise me. When she walked up she had a toddler holding her hand. I have a two-year-old, but this was not my child. At the time I was dreaming I thought it was my husband (as a child). When I woke up I remembered where I had seen the child's face. I think it was my dad as a baby. I have seen pictures of him as a child. This upset me because he is terminally ill and I felt like this was a kind of premonition. After all, she is dead and if my dad was with her that meant he would have to be dead, too. I really didn't give this much thought until I woke up.

The entire time I was dreaming I knew I was asleep. I did not want N. to go. She did not vanish at the end. She simply went back the way she came when we were finished talking. I was left with a very good, very blessed feeling. I couldn't wait to wake up and write it down. I knew before I woke up that I would need to write all of it down.

The dreams with the mother-in-law contain many elements common to dream visits with the dead. Here the mother-in-law is seen walking down a road. The dead are often first seen coming from a long way off. Crossing a bridge or a threshold may occur. Sometimes the meeting takes place in a location meaningful to both the dead and the dreamer. In other cases, the dead may appear in the bedroom.

The energy of the dream is high, and involves physical sensations. Communication is telepathic. Though the dreamer realizes she is lucid in the dream, she knows she cannot—or should not—try to control it, like other lucid dreams. The visit dream is different, and unfolds in its own way.

Afterlife dreams and near-death experiences

Afterlife dreams share many characteristics of near-death experiences (NDEs), in which an individual is taken to the edge of the afterlife during a life-threatening crisis, or during intense states of emotion and spiritual practice. Afterlife dreams involve meetings with the dead to receive messages, and also involve previews of dying and the afterlife.

Like significant dreams of the dead, NDEs have been documented since ancient times. Perhaps the earliest known account was given by Plato in *The Republic*, written around 420 BCE. NDE accounts have been recorded throughout history. According to the International Association for Near-Death Studies, surveys taken in the United States, Australia and Germany indicate that 4 to 15 percent of the population has had NDEs. The term "near-death experience" was coined in the 1970s by Dr. Raymond Moody, whose ground-breaking book *Life After Life* brought international attention to the phenomenon.

As mentioned, not all NDEs occur when a person is close to death. Some people report profound NDEs during meditation and prayer; periods of intense emotions and upheaval; waking consciousness; and sleep. NDEs during sleep overlap with afterlife dreams; in fact, it may be difficult to separate one from the other.

Significant shared characteristics between afterlife dreams and NDEs are:

Lucidity. There is a sense of having a real experience. In some cases, NDEs have a dream-like quality, or, the experiencer wonders if he is having a dream.

Travel or sudden transport to a distant location. The journey is marked by speed and light. Dreamers who preview the afterlife may not undergo the travel but abruptly find themselves in a "different" environment.

A pervasive presence of light. The journey and the environment are lit with brilliant white or golden light, and sometimes colors that are intense and defy description.

A beautiful place. The surrounding environment may be a beautiful park or garden, or a field of light.

The presence of the dead and spiritual guides. The "others" may accompany the experiencer or may appear at the destination. For dreamers, the dead may come into the environment of the living, or, the meeting takes place in a location that seems to be between worlds.

A threshold that marks the boundary between life and the afterlife. For NDErs, it is a point of no return. The boundaries are sometimes recognizable symbols, such as doorways and bridges; in other cases, the line is understood. A voice or guide tells them they cannot cross because it is not yet their time, or gives them a choice to stay or return to the living.

Dreamers often see the dead arriving from a long way off, and understand that they cannot follow.

Telepathic communication. NDErs and dreamers usually communicate with the dead and guides, but via thoughts that are impressed on the mind. They may "hear" the voice.

Life reviews. NDErs often review their entire lives in a flash. Dreamers sometimes have limited life reviews of significant events they shared with the dead, a way of acknowledging the bond, and a mechanism for letting go.

Knowledge of the future. NDErs may be shown visions of the future. In many cases, they see the consequences of destructive acts for humanity as a whole. Such visions inspire a reorientation of values upon return.

For dreamers, knowledge of the future usually has a more personal context. The dead provide advice and warnings for future decisions and courses of action.

Transformation. NDErs often return to life with markedly changed values. They lose their fear of death, and the material concerns and ambitions they held before no longer have the same importance. Dream visits with the dead also have transformative power for the living, usually to move on through the grieving process, but also to reevaluate their own lives and the importance of their values and pursuits. Dreamers also may alter their views of dying and the afterlife.

Natural explanations have been advanced for both NDEs and afterlife dreams. In the case of NDEs, oxygen deprivation and releases of neurochemicals in the dying brain are suggested as causes. In the case of dreams, wish fulfillments, day residues, internal states of emotions, and dream-state telepathy (such as between the dying and the living) are given as reasons for the dreams. Experiencers, however, do not see their events as hallucinatory, imaginary or projections of emotions. They are real events, driven by a higher purpose. All of those factors may indeed play roles, but ultimately the means by which we have an extraordinary experience is far overshadowed by the experience itself, and its effect on the person.

The benefits of afterlife dreaming

Dream visits and messages from the dead can alleviate grief and facilitate closure, and should be integrated into any counseling. Visitation dreams should be evaluated for both their symbolic content and their integrity as real events.

In addition, such dreams can help the living process beliefs and concerns about dying and the afterlife. Natural concerns and questions arise throughout life, as we ponder the meaning of why we are here, where we came from, and where we are going when our time in done. Visitation dreams are direct experience, the most powerful way to acquire spiritual knowledge and wisdom.

The following chapters will discuss the foundation of dreams and afterlife dreams; the different types of afterlife dreaming and dream messages; and how we should view and integrate these special dreams.

2

Our Dream Heritage

The ancients knew dreams as a direct connection to the spiritual realms and the divine. Dreams were a gift. People did not have dreams; they were given dreams, saw dreams, or were sent dreams in answer to human need and requests for help. Dreams were external events that occupied a bridge world—what Carl G. Jung later termed the *mundus imaginalis*, or world of imagination, that unites the world of matter and the world of spirit. Imagination does not mean that dreams are unreal fantasies, but rather that the human faculty of imagination is engaged in order to perceive the dead, spiritual figures and the spiritual planes. To the ancients, the appearance of the dead or a god in dreams was their real appearance.

Dreams in the ancient world

Our Western dream heritage dates to the Sumerians, Assyrians and Babylonians, who studied dreams for omens of state and political importance and for solutions to community disputes and problems. Dream incubation—asking dreams to answer specific questions—was practiced, and correct interpretation was a skill employed by priests, seers and professional dream interpreters. In these early times, the dreams of rulers and important people were given more attention and weight than the dreams of the masses, but today we know that everyone's dreams are equally important, and are carriers of information, knowledge, truth, healing and guidance.

The oldest dream book in existence comes from Assyria: a collection of clay cylinders found at Nineveh in the library of the famous Assyrian king Ashurbanipal, who ruled from 669-626 BCE.

Dreams in ancient Egypt

The Egyptians absorbed some of the Assyrian and Mesopotamian dream practices into their own culture. They too, practiced dream incubation for guidance and divining the future, and they were visited by the gods in dreams. They believed that in sleep, humans had access to another realm not ordinarily available to them in waking life. They considered dreams to be a revelation of truth and thus attached great significance to dreams, looking to dreams alone for information about the future. The Mesopotamians, on the other hand, included dreams among many other methods of divination.

Instructions given in a dream were to be acted upon, otherwise misfortune could occur. Thus, it was of great importance to be accurate in interpreting a dream, lest the gods be angered. During Dynasty XVIII (c. 1400 BCE), a young prince was hunting in the Giza plateau near the Sphinx. He rested there, and fell asleep in the statue's giant shadow. The Sphinx sent the prince a dream in which it promised him the throne of Egypt if he would clear away all the sand that had accumulated over the Sphinx's body. The prince did as instructed. In time, he became pharaoh, Thutmose IV. He recorded the story on a stele and planted it between the paws of the Sphinx. The Dream Stele, as it is called, remains there today.

The primary interpreters of dreams and guardians of official dreamwork practices were called "lector priests." The lector priests were attached to the House of Life, an institution at most cult and some mortuary temples throughout the land. The priests were learned men who kept the sacred books containing the religious lore and laws, and magical rites. They were renowned dream interpreters. The House of Life was a building, or a small group of buildings, where the temple library was kept, and where lay people could come and receive consultation, such as dream interpretation and spells to solve problems. The dream and magical books were carefully guarded in order to protect the magical status of the priests. Besides the priests, there were scribes and literate wealthy and noble persons who were likely to possess private books of dream spells and interpretations.

Temple and private dream books were written on scrolls of papyrus and stored in boxes or jars. Fragments have survived, giving us a look at how Egyptians viewed their dreams. The earliest known fragment, called the Chester Beatty Papyrus 3, dates to the Twelfth Dynasty (2050-1790 BCE), and now is owned by the British Museum.

Dreams figured prominently in magical practices. Spells and rituals provided for "sending" dreams to another person to influence their thinking and actions. Even the dead could send dreams to the living, usually to answer questions about the future or to enforce spells. The dead were believed to have great power to intervene in the lives of the living.

Dreams among the early Hebrews

The early Hebrews placed a high value on dreams as real experiences of the direct voice of God. The Torah is replete with examples of dreams and waking visions, affirming these as primary ways that a concerned God speaks to human beings to provide direction and guidance.

There was no clear-cut distinction between dreams and waking visions, which were seen as different aspects of experiencing the nonordinary world. For example, there are references to a "vision of the night" (1 Samuel 3:15; Job 20:8; Isaiah 29:7; and Daniel 2:19 and 7:2); "in the night I saw" (as in

Zechariah 1:8); and "in the visions of my head as I lay in bed" (Daniel 4:13), which probably refer to dreams.

The tradition for God to address prophets through dreams is established in Numbers 12:6, when God tells Moses, Miriam and Aaron, "Hear my words: If there is a prophet among you, I the Lord make myself known to him in a vision, I speak with him in a dream."

Many other Biblical prophets, patriarchs and rulers were inspired and directed by dreams or visions, among them Samuel, Saul, Solomon, Elijah, Jeremiah, Job, Isaiah, Ezekiel and Daniel. Their experiences include the voice of God, the appearances of angels, and visions of heaven. These "big" dreams were the instruments by which God spoke to the people.

The importance of dreams is emphasized in other Jewish sacred texts as well. The Talmud, a body of rabbinical teachings based on the Torah and put in written form between 200-500 CE, encourages paying attention to dreams. Professional dream interpreters were respected and paid for their work.

Talmudic interpreters relied upon scripture, but did understand the personal and subjective nature of dreams. Nearly all of the interpretations offered in the Talmud are positive, because it was the job of the dream interpreter to help the client release anxieties, much the same approach we take today.

The reverence for dreams continued on through the Middle Ages. The Zohar, a Kabbalistic text written down by Moses de Leon, declares that everything that happens is made known first through a dream or proclamation: "Nothing takes place in the world but what has previously been made known, either by means of a dream, or by means of a proclamation, for it has been affirmed that before any event comes to pass in the world, it is first announced in heaven, whence it is proclaimed to the world." Thus, dreams have value for humanity.

The Sefer Hasidim, credited primarily to Judah ben Samuel, distinguishes between dreams during sleep and visions during waking consciousness, though both are channels of communication between the living and the dead.

In the 16th century, an important text on dream interpretation was published by the philosopher Solomon Almoli. It was first titled *Chelmin* ("Dream Mediator") and then retitled *Pitron Chalomot* ("The Interpretations of Dreams"). Almoli described eight "gates" as a systematic way of understanding dreams. He said the dreamer's emotions are important to the interpretation. In subsequent chapters, we shall see how this is a factor that plays great significance in afterlife dream messages and meetings with the dead.

Dreams in early Greece and Rome

The ancient Greeks continued many of the dream beliefs and practices of the Egyptians, Mesopotamians and Hebrews; they, in turn, influenced the Romans. Dreams were events that were witnessed: the Greeks did not "have" dreams but "saw" them. In the earliest beliefs, the gods and the dead made real visits to the dreamer, entering a bedroom through the keyhole and standing at the head of the bed while they delivered their message. Such dreams were considered to be objective events that happened independently of the dreamer, and did not arise from within the dreamer.

Like the Hebrews, the Greeks drew little or no distinction between dreams and other kinds of visionary experiences that happened during both day and night, in sleep, trance and waking consciousness. The emphasis was on the content of the experience, and on the ability of humans to perceive and communicate with another reality.

Around the 7th century BCE, shamanic and Eastern ideas about dreams were introduced to Greek culture. Rather than being visited, the dreamer traveled out-of-body at night to a meeting place.

Plato (427?-347 BCE) called dreams the *metaxu*, the "between state," a real place where the human soul went during sleep to meet the gods, demigods and the dead who are otherwise inaccessible. He said that dreams are another way to know the world besides sense and experience; we can receive "the inspired word" of the divine in our sleep. Plato said that dreams embody the heights and the depths of human consciousness.

The Greeks had much to say about the divinatory role of dreams. The Stoic philosopher Posidonius (c. 135-150 BCE) said that dreams are a natural form of divination. They can foretell the future because in sleep the soul communicates directly with the gods or with an "immortal soul," one of the many divine beings who exist in the air beneath the moon, and who know the future. They can impart their knowledge to humans only when the soul is free of the body in sleep.

Augustus Caesar (63 BCE-14 CE) took dreams so seriously that he proclaimed a new law: anyone who dreamed about the commonwealth was required to proclaim it in the market place. Perhaps he hoped to avoid a surprise upset by the public airing of potentially prophetic dreams concerning matters of state.

Plutarch (46?-c.120 CE), a Greek historian who became a Roman citizen, reasserted the divinatory power of dreams, calling them the "oldest oracle." He said that everybody—not just selected priests and oracles—could experience prophecy in dreams.

The first known dream book in Greek dates to the 5th century BCE, and is credited to Antiphon, an Athenian statesman. The oldest surviving dream book in Greek, *Oneirocritica* ("The Study of Dreams") dates from the 2nd century, written by Artemidorus of Daldi, a Greek professional dream interpreter who spent part of his career in Rome. Artemidorus collected about 3000 dreams from his clients. He believed strongly in the benefit of understanding dreams, writing in his book that "dreams and visions are infused into men for their advantage and instruction."

Dreams in Christianity

Initially, Christianity continued the honoring of dreams and visions as a primary way that God communicates with humans. Dreams and visions literally shaped the birthing and early development of Christianity. Angels are the chief messengers of God; descriptions of them "coming" and "standing" before people are reminiscent of the Greek Homeric dreams in which gods came and "stood" by the head of the bed while they delivered a message in a dream. As in the Old Testament, distinctions are not always made between dreams and other kinds of visionary experiences.

In the early centuries, the Church Fathers, many of whom were Platonic philosophers and Greek converts, reaffirmed the tradition of God speaking through dreams and visions. Justin Martyr, Irenaeus, Clement of Alexandria, Origen, Tertullian, Athanasius, Augustine, John Chrysostom, Anthony, Basil the Great, Gregory of Nazianzen, Gregory of Nyssa, Ambrose, Gregory the Great, and John Cassian are among those who upheld dreams as a proper way to maintain contact with God.

Attitudes began to shift in the 4th century under the influence of Jerome, who translated the Bible from Greek and Hebrew into the Latin Vulgate. Jerome was raised in an affluent Christian family, but devoted himself to an intense study of the pagan classics. One night he had a realistic dream in which he was taken before God and scourged for his interest in pagan studies. He awoke with his shoulders bruised, black and blue. He got the message, and dropped all pagan pursuits, even retiring to the desert as a hermit for several years.

Despite his own dream experience, Jerome disapproved of dreams. He said that the word of God could not be sought through pagan practices of dream incubation, which was practiced in hundreds of dream temples, not only for prophecy, but for literal healing within dreams themselves.

In his Latin Vulgate Bible, Jerome made the association between dreams and "witchcraft." His translation of the Bible remained the authoritative version in Western Christianity up until the mid-20th century.

Dreams in the Middle Ages onward

Even before the advent of Christianity, scholars of all faiths had debated the truth and reality of dreams. There were skeptics in the ancient world, just as there are today. Chief among them was Aristotle (384-322 BCE), a pupil of Plato's, who argued that the world and existence can only be known through the physical senses.

The medieval theologians of Christianity found little to no favor in dreams. In the 13th century, Thomas Aquinas (1225-1274), one of the greatest scholars of the Christian church, added to the decline of the dream by supporting the Aristotlean view, which he believed would modernize the Church. He could not, however, dismiss Biblical tradition, and so acknowledged that some dreams come from God.

Interestingly, Aquinas, like Jerome, had life-changing dreams or visionary experiences that altered the course of his work. During his composition of his great work, *Summa Theologica*, he struggled with completing a theological passage. One morning he suddenly dictated it with ease. He told his scribe that he had had a dream in which he dialogued with the apostles Peter and Paul, and they told him what to say.

Aquinas had a profound impact on the subsequent development of Western thought toward dualism, skepticism, behavioralism and rationality. For example, Renee Descartes (1596-1650) supported the Aristotlean view. Like Aquinas, he thought dreams to be merely the products of food eaten. And, like Jerome and Aquinas, he disparaged dreams yet was influenced by them himself. One of Descartes's most important philosophical works, *Discourse on Method* (1637) was inspired by a dream.

Though dreams fell in importance, they continued to serve a purpose for the Church in its efforts to spread the doctrine of purgatory. Dreams of the unhappy dead in purgatory were used as teaching examples for adhering to church doctrine.

The Reformation of the 16th century brought an end to widespread belief in miracles and supernatural events. By the 18th century, the dream was nearly finished as a spiritual experience. Dreams would not return to importance in the West until the 20th century.

Psychology reclaims the dream

New life was breathed into the dream by the emergence of psychology. In his pioneering work, *The Interpretation of Dreams* (1900), Sigmund Freud (1856-1939) said dreams were the "royal road" to the unconscious. He had a narrow view of them, however, considering them wish fulfillments of repressed infantile desires, "day residues" from daily life, and fantasy. He said dreams have little practical importance, and are part of pathology. His pupil Carl G. Jung (1875-1961) disagreed, and restored dreams to their ancient importance, but for a modern audience.

Jung considered dreams to be the expression of contents of two types of the unconscious: the personal unconscious, which relates to personal experience, and the collective unconscious, which is the repository of human beliefs and experiences collected throughout history, shared by all people. The purpose of dreams is compensatory: to provide information about the self, achieve psychic equilibrium or offer guidance. Jung believed that dream symbols from the collective unconscious have universal, or archetypal, meanings, but those from the personal unconscious do not, and take on meaning from the individual's experiences, beliefs and cultural, racial, ethnic and religious heritage.

Jung developed his concept of archetypes from the foundation laid by the Greeks. The philosopher Heraclitus (535-475 BCE) was the first to view the psyche as the archetypal first principle. Plato articulated the idea of archetypes in his Theory of Forms, which holds that the essence of a thing or concept is its underlying form or idea.

Archetypes appear in myth, legend and folk tales. They are primordial images of unknown origin that have been passed down from an ancestral past that includes not only early man but humanity's prehuman and animal ancestors. Archetypes are not part of conscious thought, but are predispositions toward certain behaviors. They are endless, said Jung, created by the repetition of situations and experiences. God, birth, death, rebirth, power, magic, the sun, the moon, the wind, animals and the elements are archetypes, as well as are traits embodied in the hero, the sage, the judge, the child, the trickster and the earth mother. Associations, symbols, situations and processes are archetypes.

Archetypes are charged with a mysterious, transcendent power, and demand to be taken seriously. They are a force in dreams, especially "big" dreams involving spiritual messages and contact with otherworldly realms.

For his insights into dreams, Jung drew from the well of his own rich, visionary dream experiences. From early in life until the end, he had many dreams that were full of alchemical, mythical, archetypal and transcendent symbols. He recorded 42 of these in his autobiographical *Memories, Dreams, Reflections*.

Jung became increasingly unsettled about what he perceived as Freud's inability to recognize deep the symbolic contents in Jung's own dreams. Freud, however, could not get past his conviction that wish fulfillment was the driving force for all dreams.

After the break with Freud, Jung went through a tumultuous six-year period often described as a breakdown characterized by psychotic fantasies, but which was more of a breakthrough to a new understanding of consciousness. He was way beyond his time, and was labeled a "mystic"—not a complimentary term back then—for his unusual ideas. He was shunned by his peers.

This phase was a productive one for him, incubating many of the ideas that he would spend the rest of his life developing. Jung experienced numerous paranormal phenomena, and vivid dreams and visions. The distinction between his dreams and visions faded, and he later recorded episodes of both in detail. He became immersed in the world of the dead, which led to his inspired writing of *Seven Sermons to the Dead*, penned under the name of the second-century Gnostic writer, Basilides, and published in 1916. Jung described the spirits of the dead as "the voices of the Unanswered, Unresolved and Unredeemed."

Three days before he died, Jung had the last of his visionary dreams, and a portent of his own impending death. In the dream, he had become whole. A significant symbol was tree roots interlaced with gold, the alchemical symbol of completion. When he died at his home in Zurich on June 6, 1961, a great storm arose on Lake Geneva and lightning struck a favorite tree of his.

Jung's contributions to our understanding of consciousness, dreams and the striving for psychic integration and wholeness continue to provide the foundation for most modern dreamwork.

Modern approaches to dreams

Since Freud and Jung, other theories have been put forward on the nature, function and meaning of dreams. Until about the 1970s, the interpretation of dreams was still left to professionals, the psychologists, psychiatrists and therapists who replaced the ancient dream priests and oracles.

In the ensuing years, lay dreamwork has become popular, and provides individuals with many benefits. Ordinary dreams address our daily and emotional concerns. Spiritual dreams take us into a cosmic arena, where we return, once again, to that "between place" described by Plato where we meet God or the divine, spiritual beings, and the dead.

The dreamscape extends far beyond into reaches we may not even comprehend. It exists beyond the limits of time and space, incorporates past, present and future simultaneously. This timeless realm corresponds to the Dreamtime of the Australian Aborigines from which continually arises the material world, like a dream of the universe.

In the terms of quantum physics, the dreamscape emerges from the implicate (folded) order, the seamless whole of the universe, the unbroken continuum of all things. Like the Dreamtime, it is a deep level of reality that contains all time and yet is timeless. It holds all potentiality. It is fluid. From the implicate order comes the explicate (unfolded) order, which is what we know as material reality. There is a constant flow of energy between the two orders. There is no cause-and-effect, but rather influences that give rise to the connections called synchronicity. Our dreams penetrate the implicate order.

Dreams as exceptional human experiences

Many of the dreams we experience, including afterlife dreams, are more than dreams. In parapsychology these types are called "exceptional human experiences" (EHE). The term was coined in 1990 by Rhea A. White to describe a wide range of anomalous, nonordinary and (at present) inexplicable experiences reported by people. White defined 150 types of exceptional experiences.

White's ground-breaking research in this area was motivated by her own near-death experience (NDE), which occurred in 1952 in an automobile accident that killed the friend she was riding with. In 1978, White co-authored a book, *The Psychic Side of Sports*, with Michael Murphy, co-founder of the Esalen Institute in Big Sur, California. The book documents the exceptional experiences of athletes and sports men and women, such as ecstasy, timelessness, out-of-body experience (OBE), supernormal perception and strength, weightlessness, and awareness of "the Other," characteristics also shared by many NDEs, lucid dreams, and afterlife dreams.

White recognized that many of these transcendent experiences have a powerful, transformative impact upon people. Beliefs about life, the afterlife, and reality can shift dramatically, for example.

For more than 35 years, White was guided by her own dreams to pursue her research in the frontiers of consciousness studies. She identified five broad categories of EHEs. Dreams, including afterlife dreams, fit all of them:

1. *Psychical*: Forms of psi (clairvoyance, telepathy, precognition, psychokinesis). Many dreams involve these elements.

2. *Death-related*: Experiences of sensing a separation of the physical and nonphysical self, especially related to one's own NDE or another person's death; also memories of between lives and the time prior to a new birth. We dream of visiting the afterworld, of having contact with the dead, and sometimes of the souls who are about to be born to us.

3. *Mystical*: Experiences of a sense of greater connection, sometimes amounting to union with the divine, other people, life-forms, objects or one's surroundings, up to and including the universe itself. We have transcendent dreams of all of these types of experiences.

4. *Encounter*: Experiences of sensing, perceiving or "knowing" the presence of an "unusual or unexpected being." In extraordinary dreams, we encounter the dead, angels, aliens, spiritual guides and masters and other nonhuman entities.

5. *Enhanced experiences*: Experiences that are at the limit of what our culture considers "normal." These involve peak experiences of emotion and transcendence, bursts of unusual mental and physical abilities, and so on. Dreams that fit here are lucid, out-of-body, miraculous healing, afterlife, and creative genius.

The three levels of dreams

To understand the essence of a dream, especially afterlife dreams, we must simply accept it for what it is—an experience in another reality. We must become dream shamans, and enter the dreamscape with the knowledge that our experiences in it are real and have their own validity and integrity.

How should we view dreams? A dream is like a diamond—it has many facets, each with its own beauty, yet part of a whole. Dreams reflect our inner state of being, and, on another level, take us to other realities which have their own integrity. Thus dreams, even meetings with the dead, can have multiple meanings:

1. *Personal*: The dream expresses a part of us, drawn from our life experiences, day residues, and emotions.

2. *Archetypal*: Some elements in a dream express archetypal energy from the collective unconscious. These images exist in their own right in the dream and must be experienced as such. Archetypes can act as messengers in dreams.

3. *Transpersonal*: Dreams are experiences of cosmic consciousness, in which creation is revealed to us. The boundaries of time and space disappear. We see the past, the future and the ever-present now. We see into other realms, such as the afterlife of the dead and the kingdom of angels. We hear the voice of God. We are linked to the consciousness of all beings.

Our dreams involving the afterlife and the dead carry special meaning and power on all three of those levels. The next chapters discuss the most common types of afterlife dreams.

3

Farewell Dreams

Janet's father died after a long illness involving a great deal of chronic pain. The toll taken by the pain showed on his face and wore his energy down. Nonethless, he seldom complained, because he did not want to worry his family. Said Janet:

> On the night my father died, I had a dream of him. I was in the habit of praying for him before going to sleep. As I drifted off with my eyes closed, I suddenly had a crystal clear image of him. It was just his face. But instead of looking haggard and worn, he looked radiant and even youthful. He said, "I am not in pain anymore." Then his face rose up and went out of sight.
>
> The dream jolted me awake. I had a peculiar feeling, and wondered if Dad had died. In the early morning I received word that Dad had died peacefully in his sleep. I was able to ascertain that he had passed away at about the time of my dream. I had looked at the clock when I came awake.

When people depart the physical plane, they send out a great burst of energy as they shed the body and take on a new form. The intensity of this burst varies considerably, depending on the condition of the dying and the circumstances of their death. In expending the energy, they may be able to have farewell visits, even to distant persons, to pay a final good-bye.

In the late 19th and early 20th centuries, psychical researchers who were looking for evidence of survival after death collected and studied farewell visits, or "crisis apparitions." They also studied non-death-related crisis apparitions, involving living persons who were undergoing a severe crisis and unconsciously projected their double to another person.

Characteristics of farewell visits

Farewell visits share a number of consistent characteristics that are documented in anecdotal accounts and psychical research literature. Not every farewell dream features all of them.

Timing and duration

Farewell visits usually occur at or near the time of death, or within about 12 hours. In some cases, there is a greater time lag, such as in dreams involving a death that occurred earlier in the day or up to about two days before.

The appearance of the dying is brief, especially if it occurs during waking consciousness. In those cases, the experiencer may suddenly see the person standing next to them or near them in the room. They may see them actually enter the room, and think that the person has physically come in. The vision of the dying person fades away. Understandably, many people are so startled by it—especially if they know the other person is far away—and think the image is their imagination.

Farewell dreams also are short. They have the same hallmarks as afterlife visits: lucidity, clarity, unusual atmosphere, and tactile sensations. In some cases, people awaken from sleep to see the person at the foot of the bed.

Appearance

The dying are usually seen full-bodied, or, like the dream above, in partial form. They seem real and solid. They appear as they did in their final moments, wearing the garments they had on when they died.

June's mother was 97 years old and in reasonably good health, but an accident brought the beginning of the end. She fell and broke her hip. A hip transplant was successful, but Helen had to leave her apartment home and enter a nursing home, where she was very unhappy. She kept talking about wanting to "go home." At first, June thought she meant her old apartment, but it then dawned on her that Helen was talking about going home to heaven. Helen lasted two months in the nursing home and then died comfortably in her sleep. Said June:

> When Mother was at the nursing home, they wrapped her legs in some kind of white stockings. I remember seeing them on her but didn't pay much attention to the details. On the morning of her death, I awakened about six or seven, but was not wholly awake. It was more like a borderland state between sleep and wakefulness.
>
> As I lay on my back, I "saw" Mother's body superimposed on mine, as though we were the same person, yet I knew we weren't. Then her body, transparent, and wearing those white stockings, began to rise from my body. The words "Mother's rising, Mother's rising" came to my mind.
>
> A couple hours later, I got the call from the nursing home that Mother had passed away.

If the dying were killed suddenly in an accident, warfare or by violence, they may show their fatal injuries, torn clothing, and sad or shocked expressions. One of the cases collected by psychical researcher F.W.H. Myers in *Human Personality and Its Survival of Bodily Death* illustrates these characteristics:

Before he went off to combat, Oliver and his brother, Russell, made a light-hearted pact that if anything should happen to Oliver, he would appear in Russell's room to let him know. On the night that Oliver was fatally shot in the head, Russell awakened to see his brother kneeling in the room, surrounding by a phosphorescent mist. He was silent, and looked sadly and lovingly at Russell. He turned his head, and Russell saw a wound on his right temple with red streaming from it. Russell was so shaken that he left the room. Later he received word about his brother's death.

The following dream farewell has similar features. Patti's younger brother, Bill, was killed late one night in an auto accident. Patti no longer lived at home, and had no knowledge of her brother's activities or whereabouts. On the night of his death, she had an unusual dream:

> He looked very strange. His shirt and jeans were ripped and blackened and his face was streaked with what looked like blood. His arms hung at funny angles. I thought he was playing a joke on me, dressed up with make-up. But he looked at me very solemnly and said he was leaving, he had to go somewhere.
>
> When I woke up, I didn't know what the dream meant, but it left a big impression on me. I knew something wasn't right. My mother called early in the morning to give me the news about Bill's accident.

Others who have gone through long terminal illnesses, especially involving intense pain, may look radiant and at peace. Still others may convey that nothing is wrong—they are just passing through or dropping by.

Speech

The dying may speak a few words or remain silent. Some give a farewell gesture. Some of the fatally wounded silently point to their injuries. If they speak, their voices sound natural and are recognizable to the experiencer.

In dreams, the communication may be conveyed telepathically rather than verbally. The dreamer may "hear" words but notice that lips do not move.

In *Phantasms of the Living*, psychical researchers Edmund Gurney, F.W.H. Myers and Frank Podmore related a case in which a woman dying of heart disease appeared in a dream to her daughter, who was in a distant location. She embraced her daughter fervently and said, "Don't cry, don't feel badly, you have done everything you could for me." The daughter felt her touch and heard the words. In the morning, she announced that she had to visit her mother, who must have taken ill. Before she could leave, she received word of her mother's death.

An interesting twist in the case is that the dying woman's daughter-in-law was at her bedside when she passed. Her final words were, "Don't cry, don't feel badly, you have done everything you could for me."

Permission to die

Peaceful dying is not always easy. Caregivers know how strongly the feelings of the living can influence the dying process. Unresolved problems, unfinished business, and loved ones who don't want someone to die can all contribute to delaying the dying and adding to the discomfort of the one who is about to pass on. A dying person often comes to terms with death before loved ones do. However, once impending death is accepted, it is important to the dying to make the transition as peacefully as possible, and with the support of loved ones.

Even when a dying person is comatose, they still can be aware of impending death on some level of consciousness. They can also be aware of what others around them are saying, thinking and feeling. Knowing that loved ones are suffering great distress can influence the dying to hold off death as long as possible.

In *Final Gifts: Understanding the Special Awareness, Needs, and Communications of the Dying*, authors and hospice nurses Maggie Callanan and Patricia Kelley tell of numerous cases they witnessed in which peaceful dying could not be completed until the right circumstances were in place, including permission to die from others. The permission could be indirect, such as in assurances that "everything will be fine" or "it's all right to go." When the right permission is given, a peaceful death often quickly follows.

"Please let me leave"

Lillian H. had a dream about the need to let go of her terminally ill mother, who could not die while Lillian was holding on with great emotional intensity.

Spiritually gifted from childhood, Lillian sees the dead and spiritual guides. She can feel the touch of invisible guides and hear them call her name. She described her experience:

> I always have loved my God, and I was reared in the Catholic church. I taught catechism to young children. I have always worked, first as a practical nurse, then as a pre-school teacher, and currently as an administrative assistant at a university. My life has not been easy, but I have always kept my faith, and I guess that's what keeps me going. Now I feel compelled to tell about an event that is very personal to me.
>
> My dear mother, may God bless her soul, was diagnosed with cancer in the left hemisphere of her brain. The doctors told me to talk with my peers, because she needed surgery immediately. The doctors said that if we agreed to surgery, she might survive nine months. If we didn't, she might survive three months. My peers and I agreed on the surgery.
>
> Within three months of the surgery, the radiation treatments started causing her seizures which left her paralyzed and speechless. Finally the cancer took her whole brain. I would run from work, run home to cook for my family, and rush to the hospital every day.
>
> Then one night, when I went to the hospital, the doctors were waiting for me. They wanted to talk to me regarding her impending death. They felt that we were suffering too much, and that if she should go into cardiac arrest or respiratory failure, I should sign the forms allowing them not to put her on a machine or to resuscitate her. I called my sister from the

nurses' station. She was hysterical on the phone. Finally, she agreed that I should sign the papers.

Immediately after that, I requested a Catholic priest to come and give my dear mother her last rites and blessings. As I stood there with the priest, praying while he blessed her, all I could see were deep tunnels in her eyes. When we finished, the priest told me that my mother was dead, but her soul would not leave her body because she didn't want to leave me and my peers. He said that I should find it in my heart to give her permission to leave and allow her to go.

"Father," I said in tears, "I can't do that."

He said I must find the way to let her go. He walked with me out of the hospital.

When I got home, I called my sister and, crying, explained what had happened. I asked her if she could find it in her heart to allow my mother to leave us. Crying, she said she could not. That night, I went to sleep and had this dream:

I had gone to the hospital to visit my mother as usual. When I went to get the elevator, some nurses and doctors were running because there had been a cardiac arrest. Intuitively, I knew it was my mother. However, when I got to her floor and I reached her door, instead of her private room, I was in a room full of beds with people who were dying.

I looked for my mother until I found her. She was in a bed, yet she was fenced in with a door on the top. When I looked at her, she was completely naked on the bed. She turned her head towards me and she said, "God bless you, my daughter."

I said, "Mommie, what are you doing here, naked?" She said, "Please my daughter, let me go, open up this door and let me go." She stood upright on her tiptoes, with her arms extended towards the ceiling, and she said, "Please, Lillian, help me to go!"

I took her out of the bed, because I feared she would fall. But again, she stood on her tiptoes, with her arms extended toward the ceiling and said, "Please, my daughter, help me to leave, please let me leave."

At that point, I woke up hysterical.

Lillian was deeply shaken by the dream, but she knew what she had to do:

> The next evening, I went to the hospital after work. I knew that I had to allow her to leave. I took my prayer book and started praying. When I finished praying, in tears, I told her that we loved her and we would always love her. I explained that she had to leave this life, because her physical body was no longer good. I explained that her spirit would be going to a place where she would feel no pain. I told her that when she left her body, she should go towards the light, go into the tunnel and follow that light. I told her there would be other spiritual guides and angels that would be waiting for her. I told her I would always love her and never forget her and that someday we would be together again. That was the hardest thing I have ever done in my life.
>
> The next night, the doctors called me at 4 AM to tell me that my mother had died in her sleep, and that she did not suffer in her death. When we went to the hospital to see her, she looked so peaceful, and I knew she had found that peaceful place with God.

One explanation for Lillian's dream is that her deep distress became dramatized as a "visit" from her mother. Lillian knew what she must do, but the advice was externalized through the figure of her mother, making it more acceptable to her.

Another explanation is that Lillian had a true encounter with her mother, made possible by the interdimensional reality of dreams. Though paralyzed and speechless in her body, her mother retained an awareness that could still reach out to communicate with Lillian in a reality that was not bounded by time, space and physicality. The mother accepted her impending death and was more than ready to go, but the energy of family resistance literally held her back.

The medium of communication was the dream, and so the imagery carried the symbolism characteristic of dreams. The mother was in a cage (the reluctance of family to let go) with a door on top (the path of ascent of the spirit to the afterlife). She was naked, symbolizing her readiness to be birthed into a new existence. She was among other souls about to make their transitions.

For Lillian, a vivid encounter in the dreamscape made it possible for her to take the final step of releasing her mother without further delay.

"You can let go"

Valerie is a volunteer at a nursing home. Once a week she visits with patients, playing games, reading stories, talking with them and enjoying other social activities. Some of the patients she gets to know over a long period of time, and some come and go quickly. One of her favorites was Dorothy, who appeared in a dream at the time of her passing:

> Dorothy, who was in her eighties, and I had many pleasant visits, during which she shared information about her life and her family. Then her condition worsened, and she became terminal. Some of her family came to spend time with her. Whenever I stopped by, they were with her. Not wanting to intrude, I stayed away. But I missed her and wanted to see her, especially if she were going to die.
>
> So, one day, I went in her room, even though family was there. She recognized me and said, "Oh, I'm so glad to see you!" She held out her hand. I took her hand and sat with her awhile. She held my hand the whole time, as though she didn't want to let go.
>
> A week or so later, I had a vivid dream about Dorothy. I awoke in the middle of the night with the sensation that she was gripping my hand, as she had done the day I visited. She didn't want to let go. I got up and went to the bathroom, all time feeling that she was still hanging on to me. I felt agitated and distressed.
>
> When I went back to bed, something prompted me to say, "It's okay, Dorothy, you can let go." I kept saying that and eventually I calmed down and went back to sleep.
>
> The next time I went to the nursing home, I learned Dorothy had

passed away the night I had this experience.

Valerie was puzzled why Dorothy would reach out to her instead of a family member if she was having difficulty letting go. She obviously had been close to her family, and they were quite attentive to her during her stay in the nursing home. Perhaps she had developed a special fondness for Valerie.

Valerie acknowledged that she is psychically sensitive and has had numerous visionary and psychic experiences throughout her life. This factor may have made it easier for Dorothy to reach her than members of her family. The hand-holding session may have been a preparation for Dorothy's transition, as the memory of it made Valerie realize what was happening.

Valerie had a similar dream experience involving a writer she admired but never met:

> Roberta [a pseudonym] was an author I liked to read. I never met her, but I read some of her stories to Edna, one of the residents at the nursing home. Edna enjoyed the stories so much that I decided to write Roberta and tell her. She very graciously wrote back and sent me a couple of her books. I started following her blog and eventually learned she had developed cancer. She kept writing her blog and sharing her illness.
>
> Soon it became evident that she was close to dying. She didn't want to give up, though. She kept hanging on.
>
> During this time, my husband and I went to the shore for a vacation. I kept thinking about Roberta and checking her blog to see how she was doing. One night, I had a dream about her. She was really struggling. I "told" her that it was okay to let go. I kept telling her that. When I woke up, I felt a sense of peace.
>
> The next time I checked her blog, I learned she had passed away at about the time I had the dream.

Once again, Valerie wondered why she would have such a significant dream about someone she did not know personally. She admired Roberta's work and followed her blog—but so did thousands of other fans.

"I think my emotional involvement has a lot to do with these kinds of experiences," Valerie said. She liked Roberta's work, admired the author, and became emotionally invested in her fight against terminal illness. Roberta's sharing of her personal life and crisis on the internet is an example of the enormous power of social media to bond far-flung people together.

However, emotional connection does not automatically enable farewell or post-death communication. "There are times when I am emotionally involved and nothing happens," said Valerie. "Edna is an example. She and I became good friends and shared many visits and books and activities for seven years. I always thought that when Edna passed away I would know it. Yet, I didn't. There have been others at the nursing whom I expected to 'hear' from when they passed away, but I haven't.

The divine works in many unusual ways. Sometimes we are summoned to act as angels and guides to aid others—even people we have never met. We always rise to the task, often without realizing it until after the fact. Even then we may never fully know all the reasons why we were called.

4

Reassurance Dreams

Alan left his home one Saturday morning at his wife's request to go to the grocery store and pick up a few items for breakfast. The store was only a few miles away. He never reached it. En route, he was struck head-on while going around a curve by a driver who was texting on his cell phone and crossed over the center line. Alan died at the scene, leaving behind his wife, Robin, and their toddler daughter.

Robin suffered a deep shock that continued long after Alan's funeral. Despite the circumstances of the accident, she shouldered all the blame. There was no real need for Alan to go to the store that morning, she told herself. Why had she insisted? Adding to her emotional burden was the fact that for some time prior to the accident, the couple had been going through a rough time and strained relationship. Robin also blamed herself for all the unresolved issues and feelings. Alan was gone, and she wanted desperately to go back in time and rewrite events.

Counselors and therapists are called in to help survivors such as Robin deal with the rocky road of grief. Some survivors have profound dream visits from the dead that add a powerful healing balm, and even help them turn a corner in their own recovery.

For a long time, Robin cried herself to sleep and awakened in more tears. One night she had a vivid realistic dream. She was with Alan and he looked bright and happy. They were out somewhere in a garden-like landscape that was both familiar and unfamiliar at the same time. The sky was lit with an unusual light that was somehow different from sunlight. They were laughing and talking, and then it suddenly dawned on Robin that Alan was dead. At the same instant, he took her hand and looked into her eyes. His own eyes had an unusual light in them. "Don't be sad," he said. "It was all good. I'm fine, and everything will be fine for you and ___ (daughter)." Although Robin "heard" the words, it seemed as though they were impressed into her mind without actual speech. She started to speak, but Alan said, "I've got to go." She tried to hang on, but could not. Suddenly she saw a path behind Alan. He turned and moved rapidly along it until he vanished.

When Robin awakened from the dream, a sense of complete calm covered her like a blanket. Instead of crying, she felt strangely at peace.

In therapy, Robin saw the dream as part wish fulfillment and part healing. It expressed her wish to see Alan again and for their life together to resume, on a happier level. It also expressed the need to heal, and could be seen as Robin giving herself permission to heal and move forward.

Robin also felt that the dream was something more. It was an external event, and for a brief moment, she and Alan had really been reunited. She had felt the touch of his hand. She could recall every vivid detail. She did not know how it happened, but the dream had been a true gift from heaven.

Alan's reassurance to Robin had a tremendous impact. She still had much to do and a long way to go in restoring balance in her life, but the dream helped her to gain a new perspective and the courage to move forward.

Dreams of reassurance are the most significant dream messages we receive from the dead. Grieving and worry are natural, but when prolonged can hinder the healing process. As much we miss the dead, we must realize that they do not want their loved ones to suffer.

Everything is okay

Bonnie McEneaney lost her husband, Eamon, in the terrorist attacks on the World Trade Center in New York City on September 11, 2001. In the aftermath of 9/11, a close friend of Eamon's, John "Jake" O'Neil, had a series of dreams about him. Said Bonnie in her book Messages: *Signs, Visits and Premonitions from Loved Ones Lost on 9/11*:

> In each of them, Jake was socializing with a group of people in a bar, restaurant, or party. Eamon would then appear primarily as an onlooker or observer. "He looked wonderful with clear eyes and a beautiful happy smile," Jake said. "He didn't talk or join in. I sensed he was there to make sure I was okay. It was nice for me because he was also able to convey that he was okay and happy. He was almost in a halo, like you would see in a Mass card. He had a certain aura and a sense of peace. I came away with the feeling that he was in the light."
>
> Jake thinks these dreams may have occurred at times when he was experiencing some kind of stress and that Eamon, who was always very protective, loyal and generous with his friends, was there to give him support and reassurance.

Reassurance dreams enable the dead to let the living know that they are all right. We may see them doing things that they enjoyed in life, such as this next dream that comforted a man who lost his grandfather:

> My grandfather was a Native American shaman. Two weeks after he died, I had a dream in which I saw him dressed in white buckskin. He was outdoors. It was so real—I could literally smell the smoke of his fire.

In the next example, a woman sends a message to her spouse via a dream to a neighbor and friend:

> Wanda and Dave lived at the end of my block. Wanda began suffering with dementia, and her health went downhill. She eventually had to go into assisted living, and Dave continued to live in the house. After a long while, Wanda passed away, and I felt real bad for Dave. They were a close couple and he was lost without her.
>
> A few nights later, I had a dream in which Wanda was dancing under the big tree in their yard. She "said" she wanted me to tell Dave that she was okay and happy now. She was very emphatic that she wanted me to tell this to Dave, so I relayed the message. He was glad to know she was really okay.

The dream may have been enabled by the neighbor's emotional bond to the couple, and her sympathy for, and empathy with, Dave in his grief.

Letting go of grief

Grieving can send a person into a tailspin. There are depression periods, thoughts of following a loved one in death, anxiety over the future, and worry about fate of the one who has died: Where did they go? Are they all right?

A lifting of darkness

A young man who lost his cousin plunged into severe depression with suicidal thoughts that were unrelieved by medication. Then a dream visit turned his life around:

> I believe very strongly that dreams are a "gateway" between realms. I have been visited by a great-aunt and two cousins via dreams. The most profound one was from my 17-year-old cousin who passed away of a con-

genital heart defect. Although we were first cousins, she was raised as if she were my little sister, because our mothers are so close.

She visited me in a dream 10 months after she crossed over, and during that period prior to her visit, I was going through a deep depression and was even having suicidally obsessive thoughts. I kept asking myself why she was taken away, when she was only third from the top of the transplant list, and all of our hopes were built up. I was even on antidepressant medication that wasn't working.

After the dream, I woke up in tears, because before she left, she hugged me and filled my body with the most intense feeling of love and compassion I have ever felt.

The depression never hit me like that again, and I threw the medication away. Three years later, my life has improved tremendously. I am making more [money], I moved to a less stressful area, and I have improved communications with my other family members. To me, this is proof that my cousin did indeed visit, and it was no fantasy or figment of my imagination.

When intuition tells us our experience in a dream is real, we should accept the wisdom, which enables us to benefit from the power of experience.

No more worry

Linda T. was deeply saddened by the death of her grandfather. A dream helped her to accept his death and move through the grieving process:

My grandfather died of emphysema and watching him die, as you can imagine, was very hard. I was getting married on May 16. My grandfather died on May 3, 13 days before my wedding. I took it very hard, because I had made special arrangements for him in the church—he was going to have the best seat in the church!

My wedding came and it was a beautiful warm sunny day! I just knew my grandfather had something to do with it! I knew he was smiling down on me and the whole family. My grandfather loved to get the whole family together, there wouldn't be a minute of that time without a smile on his face.

A few weeks after my marriage I sat down and wrote him a letter, a letter I should have written him years ago. I just wanted him to know that I loved him and wanted to tell him things I should have told him while he was alive. Needless to say, I cried through the whole thing.

That night after crying myself to sleep, I dreamed of my grandfather. It was one of the strangest dreams I have ever had to this day. One wall of the bedroom looked like a movie screen, and it was showing me a movie of my grandfather when I was a very small child. He was at the lake in his bathing trunks, holding the raft for one of us to get on. He called to me, and as I looked at him he told me, "Linda, don't worry, I am all right and I am happy." I laid back down. When I woke up in the morning I was finally able to accept his death.

I believe to this day that my grandfather came to me in my dream to let me know that he was finally okay, and that I had nothing to worry about.

The number 13 played a big part in my grandfather's life. He was in the war, he was stationed on a boat—number 13. On the 13th day on the 13th hour, his ship was hit and went down. Only 13 men survived—my grandfather being one of them. My father was born on October 13 and in the end, my grandfather died 13 days before my wedding. His birthday was May 1 and he died on May 3, but those two numbers put together are 13.

I think of him often and wish he would come back to me in my dream, but I know he is watching over me and my family and that he is happy and healthy in heaven.

Linda's exercise of writing the letter prior to going to sleep may have facilitated the dream visit. She was able to move past sadness and concern about her grandfather.

Prolonged grief

Most dream visits with the dead occur within a few weeks of death, but some can occur years later. Prolonged grief may trigger a visitation dream. About two years after her father died, Shirley L. had this dream experience:

> My identical twin and I were riding in an open motorized vehicle of some sort down a street in my home town with my father's casket in the back opened. We were conversing with him while riding around and I asked him, "How can this be, Dad, you are dead."
>
> He answered, "I am always with you, Sissy, though my body is not."
>
> We continued reminiscing as we drove around my home town. The dream was in color, though I usually don't dream in color. I remember beginning to cry while still with him and crying and crying until I was crying aloud, which finally awakened me.

The dream was an expression of Shirley's profound grief. The message from her father, that he was always with her, contained the seeds for healing. Six years later, Shirley still missed her father intensely, however. She tried to contact him through the ancient technique of scrying, or gazing into a darkened mirror. She did not see him in the mirror, but the exercise paved the way for another dream encounter with her father:

> I was in this house, something similar to my childhood home, talking with people when through the dining room window I saw him passing by, smiling. I ran to the front door. The rooms grew dark and no one seemed to notice my leaving.
>
> I opened the door to let him in and there he stood, a picture of health as he did when I was in high school. He had on a lightweight jacket, off-white, with pleated trousers, and was full of life! Smiling, he stepped in. We went into another room and he sat on the couch while I sat by his feet, crying and telling him how much I missed him.
>
> He patted my head telling me, "Sissy, I am so happy, do not grieve for

me. I love you but would not want to come back. I am always with you."
As he continued to stroke my hair, I wept until I thought my heart would
break.

The crying eventually awakened me, leaving me with such a hole in
my heart, a longing. I knew he had come trying to comfort me since I had
been trying to contact him through mirror gazing.

Shirley felt the visits were real. "These two 'visits' stay with me to this
day," she said. "I did not induce these dreams or do anything unusual."

Once again, the father's message was to let go of grief. He reassured her
again that he was always with her.

Completion of life's plan

After the sudden death of her sister-in-law at age 49, Sharon grieved
over what she felt was a life cut short. A vivid reassurance dream helped her
realize that her sister-in-law had completed her life plan and had work to
do in the afterlife.

M. was a person who did everything to the best of her ability. She was
a very bright woman. She was passionate about many things. She was po-
litically astute. She had been a protester against the war in Vietnam, she
even broke men's legs (with their permission of course) to keep them from
being drafted. (I did not know this while she was alive—this was revealed
by my brother during her eulogy.) She was a gourmet cook—the perfect
hostess—putting flowers all around the house for your enjoyment during
your visit. Nothing was too good for you.

Educationally she had an ABD (all but dissertation) in psychology
and counseled people who were in terrible condition (psychologically)—
people on the streets, etc. She spearheaded a program to help abused
women. She and I were not really close; however, I cared for her as a family
member. She and my brother lived on the West Coast and I lived in Middle
America and then in the East.

It seemed to me that neither my brother nor she had any religious practices that they adhered to. They were more concerned with the human condition. They had many friends together and individually. Although, M. had a strong personality and could generate some negative feelings by her approach to you. She was so bright that I think it didn't occur to her that she could be intimidating with her knowledge and skills, or that you might not agree with her philosophically and could not express it as well as she could.

The dream:

I found myself on a path in a vacant lot or field that had been mowed down. The path was well worn and dusty. I was following a person with long flowing, rather voluminous dark hair. (This could describe my sister-in-law's hair—I never saw the face of the person I was following—but my interpretation of it was that it was my sister-in-law.)

This person was walking at a fast pace. I was trying to catch up with her. We approached a house—a little white bungalow. She went in and I followed. In the house there were many ladies dressed in silken robes with turbans on their heads—the clothing was colorful, luxurious and rich looking. There was a sense was of serene beauty and reverence.

After looking around, I could not see the person I was following, so I went into the next room. This room was enormous (nothing at all like a room in a small bungalow). The room was more like a large hotel atrium, however it went up farther than I could see and it did not have a commercial feel. It had a solemn, peaceful, reverent feeling—there was a spiral staircase all around the edges of the room and on the different levels there were people dressed in all manner of elegant robes, men and women. I got the sense that they were holy people. I looked up at them and they looked down at me.

I caught sight of the person that I was following. She was leaving the house using the back door. I followed. She quickly went down a path and into the woods. I was following her when suddenly she disappeared into the ground. This upset me terribly to see her just get quickly pulled into the earth. I began using Reiki with my hands positioned over the ground, thinking I could sense where she was and could pull her out. Nothing happened, so I kept on trying, moving around a bit.

Suddenly there rose up out of the ground a man lying on his back, eyes closed. He was wearing a beautiful blue velvet robe with a magnificent medallion on his chest. This surprised me, but I did not stop doing the Reiki over the ground, still hoping to find her. After a bit, I heard people around, and they were saying something to me. They were saying, "Thank you for bringing back Pir Vilayat Khan." I recognized the name as a Sufi leader or holy man. I wondered about this, but still wanted to look for her. Here the dream ended, or did not get retained in my memory.

I interpreted this dream to mean that my sister-in-law was meant to do important spiritual work in the world and would be reborn again soon. This thought has given me some comfort, as if she stopped short in this life so that she could complete a very important mission.

Even though the dreamer had no direct communication with the figure, she knew it was her sister-in-law. The dream includes strong symbols as well, such as the spiritual figures, the blue robe (the color of spirit), and the spiral staircase, which conveys an ascent to a higher plane of existence. Going into the earth suggests a time of incubation, gestation, or preparation, a time of being out of reach.

Restored to health

People who die of illness and injury return in dreams to let others know they are restored and well. The dead, through dreams and mediumistic communications, relate that the afterlife responds to thoughts and intentions. The dead can shape an astral body, restoring their wholeness and youthfulness.

A missing leg returns

Jerri B. had this dream after her beloved grandfather passed away:

He had had one of his legs amputated due to complications of diabetes a couple of years before he died. In the dream he was jumping up and down, clicking his heels together and looking so happy. He told me that he was very happy because he was with my grandmother and my mother, and he said to me, "See, I have my leg back too!"

Reassurance dreams usually happen once, but in some cases, multiple appearances are made until the living accept the message. In the next case, the appearance of a deceased young man changes as he experiences healing in the afterlife.

Healed and moving on

Donna Wolfe Gatti, a medium in Hedgesville, West Virginia, experienced dream visits from Jason, the teen-aged son of friends of hers. Jason died from injuries he sustained while riding a three-wheeler all-terrain vehicle. He was in a coma for 13 months and Donna spent a great deal of time with his parents during his illness. Their long wait, which ended in Jason's death, took a heavy emotional toll. Donna related:

> After Jason died, he came to me in a dream and said, "Tell my parents I'm okay." I called his mother and gave her the news. There was a long silence on her end of the line. She didn't say anything other than goodbye and I wondered if she appreciated the call.
>
> Three weeks later, Jason came to me again, in another dream, and said the exact same words. So I called his mother and told her what happened. Again, she said nothing.
>
> There were differences between the two dreams. In the first dream, Jason was wearing the head brace that he had worn during his stay in the hospital and he seemed very anxious, as if he really needed to contact his parents to let them know that he was safe. In the second dream, the brace was gone and Jason looked healthier, happier and much more relaxed.
>
> About a year later his mother asked if Jason had returned to visit me.

I said that he had not come to me in my dreams, but I would try to contact him. I searched the spiritual realm for him, but he was gone. Spirit said he had reincarnated. Knowing that Jason was back on Earth made his mother very happy.

Guilt and forgiveness

The living often feel guilty about the death of a loved one. We may blame ourselves for something we did or did not do, wondering if we could have prevented the death, or even wondering if we contributed to it. The death of a person in a troubled relationship may cause survivors to feel a particular burden of guilt for not repairing the relationship while they had the chance. Robin's story in the opening of this chapter involved a struggle with guilt as well as grief.

In addition, there may be guilt for neglecting a relationship, for acting selfishly at someone else's expense, or for having an argument or falling out that is unresolved at the time of death. Even the guilt of not having said, "I love you" one last time can be deep and profound.

Some reassurance dreams have the purpose of conveying forgiveness and understanding.

Making peace

A woman who felt she manipulated her inheritance had a dream visit of forgiveness:

I had walked down a long, dark corridor and was standing under a light centered in a hub with corridors branching out in all directions. As I looked back from where I had come, I saw a figure wearing a long black robe and hood. A monk. I kept thinking I should go back down there, but could not bring myself to do it.

Then the figure came toward me and when it was close the person threw out her arms and smiled at me. I recognized her instantly, for it was my late Aunt M. after whom I was named. Her message was that she loved me and forgave me.

For what? For being nice to her when she was alive because I had an ulterior motive. I wanted to inherit her small estate, and I did.

M. is now my spirit guide, my guardian angel who comes to me in times of need. Strangely, she is my daughter's protector, too. Strange because during her lifetime children annoyed her, and I didn't know my daughter even liked her.

The dream enabled the woman to make peace with herself and with the dead aunt, with the relationship between them taking an unexpected turn.

The continuing presence of the dead varies. In some cases, the dead move on out of reach. In other cases, they remain close to the living, and even take on roles comparable to guardian angels. The living should not try to force a continuing presence, which does not serve the best interests of either the living or the dead. We cannot second guess the needs of the dead in their new environment.

Journey to the afterlife

In the next case, a woman received a descriptive farewell dream from her mother, followed by a reassurance dream of love:

The night immediately preceding my mother's death (we had to remove her off of life support) I dreamt that she was boarding a plane and I wanted to go along but she told me I couldn't (very unusual since we did everything together). She was accompanied by a soldier and other people. Interestingly enough, the other people were fuzzy images, lots and lots of them (thousands?). I couldn't see their faces.

After she had died, exactly one month later, I did see her in a very lucid way. She was very bright and in a cocoon type of thing. I felt like I was in a place I couldn't stay. It was very bright and warm. She was in a white, sleeveless dress and kept telling me (without words, only feelings) that she loved me.

I think the soldier represented a death too soon. I thought my mother, though 74 years old, was too young to die.

I had another dream about her in which she was in her bedroom behind closed doors. I tried to open the door but I wasn't able to. She said that was okay, that I couldn't come in but that I could still talk to her through the door.

The imagery of the dream contains symbols that reinforce the messages of the visitations. The airplane and the soldier are modern versions of the means of traveling to the land of the dead. The Greeks envisioned the underworld surrounded by rivers. The dead had to be ferried across the River Styx in a boat steered by the ferryman Charon. Other symbols are black horse-drawn coaches, hearses and black automobiles, both of whom have driver escorts.

The cocoon is an image of gestation for rebirth, and perhaps represented a transition time of rest for the deceased mother.

Barriers between the living and the dead are common in dreams. In the first dream, the daughter recognizes she is in a place not meant for the living. In the second dream, she and her mother are separated by a closed door, which symbolizes the inaccessibility of the afterlife by the living. The mother's room is the bedroom, a symbol of private space. Despite the barriers, the dream message conveys the possibility for communication.

It was time to go

Stacy B. had a vivid dream about her grandmother that helped to relieve her feelings of guilt:

I am a 31-year-old single mother. After my divorce, I began a spiritual quest. I began reading everything I could get my hands on about angels, near-death experiences and religions of all kinds. In my studies, most all of the concepts were extremely easy for me to grasp. It was as if I had awakened from a dream (my old consciousness) to a new reality.

My soul embraced the concepts of angels, an afterlife, spirit guides, and being able to communicate with those who had gone on before, as if I had always known they were real and possible deep down inside, but was just now remembering them. The more I embraced these things as truth, the more experiences I had with them.

That is why when my grandmother visited me in my dreams, two days after her death, I was not at all surprised and was wholly delighted.

My grandmother died under dire circumstances. She was 86 and well nearly all the time. My father, her only child, checked on her every day to bring her dinner and make sure she was okay. But on this particular Sunday, I had come down with a terrible case of influenza. I was so faint I couldn't get out of bed, but I still had to care for my daughter. So, I called my father and asked him to care for her [the daughter]. Since he had spent the entire day with us, he did not have time to check on my grandmother. She had a massive stroke. He did not find her until the following day. The coroner told us she had laid there on her kitchen floor several hours before dying.

I was devastated. I felt like it was all my fault and I couldn't stand the thought that she lay there suffering for hours with no one to help her. And I told myself, if we had just found her, she would still be alive today.

When she came to me in the dream, it was very vivid. We were in her home and she was trying to get out the front door. She was not in her right mind, she could not talk, but just make noises. I could not reason with her. I had to physically take her back into her home and make her stay there because she was trying to "escape.", I was very frustrated and so was she. She was not the grandmother I had always known and loved.

When this sequence of the dream ended, she came to me, beautiful, peaceful and loving, and told me, "This is what I would have been like if I had lived. I would not have wanted that and neither would you."

I now knew she was happy where she was. And, I now know she did not suffer. It was her way to tell me to leave the guilt behind because things had happened the way they were supposed to have happened.

The dream conveyed a strong message to Stacy not to second-guess events, for they cannot be changed. Even if possible, such a change would have carried consequences that would have been worse. The grandmother was at peace. She wanted Stacy to be at peace as well, and not remain imprisoned by her guilt.

The dream has interesting symbolism. The house can be seen as a symbol for the grandmother's body, and the front door the place of exit for her soul. She is unable to exit her house—her body—and is frustrated at her inability to communicate. By showing Stacy the dramatic contrast between what might have happened and what did happen, the grandmother was able to set Stacy's mind at rest.

A life full circle

D. was not able to reach her dying mother before she passed away, a circumstance that happens to many people who live far away from loved ones. Guilt is a natural reaction, even if circumstances were beyond control or anticipation. In D.'s dream, a gentle life review brings solace and comfort:

> My mom passed away on January 7. A few nights after her burial, I had my dream. It was my mom's life. It was as if I was looking at a wallet photo album. All the pictures were wallet size. The first photo was when Mom was a young child. It was as if someone was flipping the photos one by one. The last photo was actually the last one taken of Mom on Christmas Day. I think Mom was telling me she had lived her life full circle.
>
> It felt like old times when I'd come for a visit and we'd look at old pictures. It was the first peaceful night's rest I'd had since Mom passed away. I really feel she wanted me to know it was time to let her go. I do remember smiling while I was viewing her life. I did not make it before she passed away (I live 1500 miles away). I kept asking her to hold on until I got there, but she just couldn't.

The dream helped the daughter to realize the blessings of her relationship with her mother. The shift in focus helped her to release guilt and work through her grieving.

Suicides

Those who take their own lives leave behind considerable grief, worry, guilt and trauma for the survivors. In addition, there are fears that the suicide dead will be condemned to eternal punishment.

Suicides sometimes make appearances in farewell and reassurance dreams, as well as in waking visions. Many mediums contact them at the request of anxious family members and friends.

The communications from suicides uphold the prevailing metaphysical concepts of the afterlife, that no supreme being judges and condemns them—they are not sentenced to a hell. Rather, they are offered the same divine love for growth and redemption that is offered to all souls. They are subject to their own life reviews, as are all souls. Their awareness and ability to grapple with their decision varies considerably: some require a great deal of rest; others are confused; some are regretful; some are not regretful. Those who have terminated their lives through assisted dying due to terminal illness also return, but express less regret for their decision.

In return visits, suicides may apologize and tell loved ones they are still loved, and not to grieve for them for they are all right. In *Love Beyond Life: The Healing Power of After-Death Communications* by Joel Martin and Patricia Romanowski, a teenage girl received a meaningful dream visit from her mother, who took her own life. Weeks after the suicide, Sandra cried herself to sleep one night and then fell into a deep sleep:

> Within minutes, she was overwhelmed by what she describes as a "beautiful aroma," the fragrance of a beautiful garden of all different kinds of flowers." Then she saw her mother surrounded by flowers. Stepping forward, she said to her daughter, "I love you, baby. I'm sorry. Don't blame yourself for anything. Mommy loves you. Forgive me. I'm fine now. Go

and be happy." After repeating the message twice, Sandra's mother walked back into the garden. Sandra continued to smell the flowers for several more minutes.

Sandra awoke feeling "very peaceful" for the first time in her life.

Like other souls in the afterlife, suicides may make a series of dream visits, changing with each meeting. In another of Anderson's cases, a young man who took his life by drug overdose returned in several dreams to his sisters. At first he looked haggard, tired and teary, but in each successive dream he became more youthful, vibrant and energetic, as though he were healing and transforming on the Other Side. In all of the dreams, he hugged the dreamer.

The special issues involved in suicide deaths and their aftermaths are dealt with in this excellent resource: *Suicide: What Really Happens in the Afterlife? Channeled Conversations with the Dead* by Pamela Rae Health and Jon Klimo.

Reunions

Lisa Krick is a paranormal investigator whose attunement to the spirit world is beneficial to her dreams. Though most reassurance dreams happen one, two or three times, Lisa is able to have occasional dream reunions with a close deceased friend.

Lisa also has had dreams where the dead ask her to convey messages of reassurance to others; she serves as an earthly contact in situations where it may be difficult for the dead to reach family directly.

> I had a dream where a family friend came to me to have me tell their kids they were okay. I wasn't even aware that she had passed yet. I had the dream and then, because the dream was so vivid and bizarre, I talked with a mutual friend of the family and found out that she had passed a couple of months prior to my dream.

I've had two other dream experiences with friends of the family who have passed away. Neither of the folks in question I had seen for years. But in both dreams I "knew" the person had passed, and they came to me to give messages of well being to members of their families. I passed along their messages.

Lisa's reunion dreams with a close friend occur during times of stress in her life. The dreams help alleviate stress and also provide comforting reassurance of her continuing connection to her friend:

I had a best friend growing up who lived down the street from me. She was two years older than me and I thought the sun rose and set on her. She died her senior year in high school. I was a sophomore. I was devastated. We'd been friends since I was five and she was seven, and when you're kids, that's a lifetime!

I needed to mourn the loss of my best friend, which included being depressed and sleeping a heck of a lot. Years passed and although I still missed her, I was finding that I thought of her less and less, as life moved on. Not necessarily a bad thing, but just the way life happens. However, there would be one song that would come on the radio that would remind me of her and make me grin and cry all at the same time. I still hear that song today and know she's with me. She's never left.

At particularly stressful times in my life, I will have a dream of the old neighborhood and me walking up to her house. In the dream, I know she's already dead, but I'll walk in the house and see her there. The rest of her family is never there ... just her ... and she'll remind me that she's passed away, and that we don't have a lot of time, but that we can visit for a little while.

And that's exactly what we do. There are no tears and no regrets in this dream, just the two of us ... talking and talking, like we used to. Then, when it's time for her to go, she smiles and goes and I wake up, completely refreshed and ready to face those trials and tribulations once more.

I've had this dream probably four or five times over the course of my life. It's extremely comforting and I'm glad I have a friend that comes back when I need her most! I have been extremely blessed to have my friend, first in life, and then in death as well. She was/is truly special.

Spiritual awakenings

The next dream carried a healing impact that remained vivid for more than 20 years for Michelle, who lost her first husband to cancer when she was 22:

> We met in high school, fell in love, moved in together just after my 15th birthday and were married when I was 17. It was a difficult life in many aspects, having to grow up so quickly, but Chris was a natural at living and all he wanted to do was play. I wanted to play too, so we were perfect for each other. He was the love of my life.
>
> The fun began to diminish when Chris started to get sick. At first I didn't believe him thinking he was just making excuses not to have to go to work. On the day he threw up blood, I knew he wasn't lying anymore.
>
> Doctors didn't believe him. Who is going to take some long haired freaky looking person seriously? Unfortunately, by the time the tumor was discovered, the cancer was in advanced stages.
>
> At first I tried to take care of him at home, giving him pain shots every three hours but it got to be too bad. He couldn't eat anymore and I watched him suffer so. After about a year and a half, I visited him in the hospital for the last time.
>
> I requested the coffin to be closed at the funeral. He weighed less than 100 pounds—a mere shadow of his brilliant beautiful self. I wanted everyone to remember him the way he was—not how he looked then.
>
> For over a year after the funeral, just before I would go to sleep, I would see that closed coffin and relive the pain of his death. Every single night. It was like a permanent event, even though I tried not to think about it, I'd lay my head down and wait for the camera to start rolling the film. I thought I was going to cry every night for the rest of my life.

Then one night I had a dream. Chris came into the bedroom and stood at the foot of the bed. He reached his hand out to me and helped me out of bed. And we walked. We walked for hours. We talked about everything. Anything I wanted to know. Then we met all our friends in a circle. Those living and passed. And they all had questions for Chris. He answered them all. We laughed and joked. It was a great time.

Then it was just him and me again. And he took me to the top of a mountain. I laid face down on the ground. He gently put his foot on my head and pointed outwards as if to give commandments to the Universe.

He said to me, "Now see.... see like the birds see." And I did. I was seeing through the eyes of birds. I was flying through the sky. And could see myself on the ground and Chris above me directing the experience. I could see things in a much different way but in many ways the same. It was a very powerful experience.

When we were finished, Chris and I walked back to my bedroom. I turned to him and asked him to take me with him. He just smiled. Without words, I could sense that he would have liked that, but he knew the Higher Plan for the both of us, so the smile was quite appropriate.

I did not make that analogy until 20 years later. After that night the funeral video no longer played in my mind before I went to sleep. Chris often comes to me now in dreams but his most favorite way of contacting me is in the form of birds cawing three times "I Love You." And today, 25 years later, I really do see things in a much different way but in many ways the same.

The dream brought not only closure to grief, but a spiritual awakening as well, with the dead serving as the guide to expanded awareness.

How to benefit from reassurance dreams

If counseling is in progress to deal with grief, bring all dreams into therapy. Even ordinary dreams in which the dead are symbolic are important to the healing process. Visitation dreams should be given special attention.

These dreams should be allowed their status as a genuine experience. It may be helpful to reenact the dream or continue it with a guided waking dream meditation. Expanding on the dream enables the dreamer to explore feelings that are not expressed within the dream.

5

Life Guidance Dreams

Meaningful dream encounters with the dead are not limited to the immediate post-death period with assurances of well-being. They can occur years later and continue to occur for years, even throughout a person's life. A dead loved one may appear at crucial times, such as when an important decision is being weighed, to offer advice and guidance, and to bestow a blessing of approval.

Advice

Dream visits are sometimes reinforced by physical evidence that removes any doubt in the mind of the dreamer about the reality of their experience. Finding a penny on the floor by the bed or in an unlikely location on the morning after a dream visit is not uncommon. The following dream visit had some unusual evidence:

Richard L. a retired aerospace quality assurance engineer, had numerous dreams of contact with relatives who died. Two experiences involving his grandfather remained vivid throughout his life. In one, his grandfather came to offer significant advice that altered the course of Richard's life.

Richard was alerted to the death of his grandfather through a psychic experience in 1947, when Richard was in the armed services.

> I was lying in bed at a disembarking center in San Francisco, talking to a bunk mate about being shipped out to Japan for occupation duty the following day. Suddenly in mid-sentence, I said that my grandfather had just died.
>
> My bunk mate, Jerry E., said "What?"
>
> I said, "My grandfather has just died."
>
> "You have got to be kidding me," Jerry said.
>
> The conversation continued while we wrote down the time and date. The next day I received a telegram that my grandfather had died the night before a few minutes before the time we had written down.

Richard was not able to attend the funeral. Three years later, his grandfather visited him in a realistic dream:

> In 1950 I was discharged and returned home to Michigan. The rooms at the old house were full of relatives, so I had to throw an old mattress down on the floor of my younger brother's bedroom to sleep. This room was my grandfather's bedroom before he died. My brother and I talked for awhile and I smoked two cigarettes, crushing the butts out in a coffee can which I placed on the table near my head. We turned out the lights and went to sleep.
>
> Sometime later I was "awakened" by my grandfather sitting on the edge of the bed in which my younger brother slept. Grandfather talked to me and informed me that I had no future in the state of Michigan. He advised me to migrate to California where my future lay. During the conversation I took the coffee can down from the table and smoked a cigarette. I don't remember all of the conversation. Then Grandpa said he had to leave. I said goodbye, and he walked out through the west wall. I

put out the cigarette and laid back down.

The next morning I awoke thinking, "What a strange dream!" Then I noticed that the coffee can with *three* cigarette butts in it was sitting beside my pillow, not on the table where I had placed it the night before.

At breakfast I told my folks about the dream. My mom asked me to describe what Grandfather had been wearing, which I did down to the silk stockings with the initial "R" in blue thread on them. My description of the clothing that Grandpa had was exactly what he had been buried in. The clothing had all been purchased new after he had died, because he didn't have anything but his overalls to wear when he lived.

I followed his instructions.

Events worked out well for Richard in California, just as his grandfather had predicted. Richard's experiences assured him of the continuity of existence on the Other Side. "I look forward to the next dimension," he said.

Take care of your son

Richard L.'s wife, Shirley (not the same Shirley L. mentioned elsewhere), had dream encounters with Richard's father, Harry, after his death:

Harry and I became very close. I didn't grow up around my father, so Harry (Dad) became more than a father-in-law. Harry lived with us for 21 years.

Dad passed away when he was 90 years old. I knew he had had a good life. He told me that he was ready to go, because he couldn't walk without a cane and he had trouble doing things. Dad would read everything he could get his hands on. He was a genius. I have never been well read. So Dad helped me to start reading and enjoying different types of literature.

I'm not sure how long after we lost Dad that he came to me in a dream. He came to me at the old farmhouse that Richard was raised in. He told me he wanted something to eat and he couldn't walk into the kitchen, so would I get him some toast and peanut butter. When I returned with his snack I found him to be about 75 years old and the cane was gone.

He asked for something to drink so I got him a cup of coffee. As I returned with the coffee I found Dad looking like he was about 50 years old. He said, "Sit down with me for awhile and talk."

I don't remember what we talked about because I was still trying to figure out how he made himself younger. After he finished his snack and coffee, he said, "Well, I had better go now. You take care of Rick and all is going to be okay for him." (Rick is my mentally handicapped son who was about 26 and still living at home. Dad knew how I worried about Rick and how he would make it in this world.)

When I became aware of being awake, I remembered all of the dream. I had a feeling that maybe things would go okay for Rick. Dad had come back to let me know that I didn't have to worry that Rick would be taken care of.

Rick is married to a handicapped girl, Mary, and they have a boy and are doing fine with help from people that know how to make their life complete.

This is another dream example of the dead finding the right dream channel for their visits. Harry did not appear to his son, Richard, who had the visit from his own grandfather. Perhaps the special emotional bond forged between Harry and Shirley opened the pathway. And, perhaps the message was more significant for Shirley, with her concern about her son.

Health matters

In the next dream, a grandmother returns to give reassurance to a child, and also to influence her health care:

I was about seven years old. My grandmother whom I had lived with the first few years of my life and was very close to had passed away. I was very ill with asthma and my doctor had been urging my mother for a year-and-a-half to send me to a special live-in hospital for children to treat this and get it under control. I really didn't want to go, having already been in and out of hospitals all my life.

One night that I'll always remember, I woke up and saw a glowing light in my room. I'm not sure if I was actually awake or dreaming, but it is still very real in my mind today. It was my grandmother standing at the foot of my bed. She told me she was all right and happy in her new home with God. Then she told me that I must go to stay in the hospital to take care of my asthma and told me not to be afraid. She said she loved me very much and that someday we would be together again. The next morning I told my mother about this and she cried. Then she made the plans for me to go into the hospital for children with asthma.

Counsel for the family

Author Ravindra Kumar described a life guidance dream, in which he was told information that was to be passed along to other members of the family:

I had a talk with my father who had expired three years earlier, through the help of a medium. After a one-hour talk, my father offered to meet me after 30 days, if it was acceptable to me. Of course, I gave my consent to him.

Exactly on the thirtieth night I dreamed of moving with my father, both of us in our light bodies, perhaps on some astral plane. The dream lasted almost about an hour in which we talked about many things of common interest. He told me many things which were to be conveyed to my mother and other relatives. We embraced each other and parted happily.

In the dream he told me that he was taking a long rest after a long time. He said that he was going to get a new body very soon and then he will be transferred to a new "more lighted region."

Blessings and assurances

Kaylie was eight years old when her favorite aunt died. At age 24, Kaylie became engaged and made plans for her wedding. She wished that her aunt could be present for the occasion.

One night she had a vivid dream in which she was with her aunt, who looked like she remembered her from childhood. The aunt wanted Kaylie to know that she approved of her fiancé and wished them a happy life.

"She was in this bright light, but she was so real," Kaylie said. "I felt like I had been transported through space and time somehow. I wanted to talk to her some more and hold on to the dream, but she smiled and turned and walked away, like she had to go somewhere. When she was talking to me, she looked so happy. I had the feeling that she was a peace."

Everything will work out

In the next dream, a deceased grandmother appeared at just the right time with encouragement and assurance. The grandmother had co-signed for her 17-year-old grandson to enlist in the U.S. Marine Corps, and then died later the same day. The two had been very close—she was always a source of spiritual faith and strength during the grandson's troubled childhood. The grandson found boot camp to be grueling. During a particularly demanding period, he had this vivid and realistic dream:

> My grandmother was standing at the stove, getting something out of the oven. I was standing near her, watching, and she spoke to me and said, "Everything will be all right." The peculiar thing to this dream was that it was so realistic and in the "now" as if the event were actually taking place; however, I was a young boy in the dream appearing to be about 9 or 10 years of age!!!
>
> I have a vivid recollection of this dream and I've shared it with my children who are now grown. I see the occurrence as an inspiration and comfort to me, and often recall it during troubling periods in my life.

The appearance of himself as a young boy may have added to the feeling of comfort in the dream. There is interesting symbolism involving the kitchen and oven. Both often represent the preparation of spiritual nourishment in dreams. The time was right, for whatever was in the oven was done.

Watching out

Sometimes dream visits from the dead occur years after the person has died, and are triggered by major changes in the lives of those still living. Jim had always been close to his mother, who died when he was in his twenties. Meanwhile, Jim married and divorced, lived alone for a while, and then remarried. One night his new wife had a lucid dream in which she "awakened" to see Jim's mother standing at the foot of the bed on Jim's side. She said, "Tell Jim I'm watching over him."

"I didn't have the feeling that she disapproved of me," said the wife. "In fact, I've always had the opposite feeling, that wherever she is, she approves. I did have the feeling that she had wanted to say that to Jim for a long time, and finally got through."

Warnings

Since ancient times, the dead have been believed to possess knowledge of the future, and to appear in dreams is to impart warnings. In the 1st century BCE, the Roman philosopher Cicero told the story of a man named Simonides, who buried a stranger. Later, as he prepared to sail away on a voyage, the dead man appeared to him in a dream and warned him not to go. Simonides decided against going, and then learned that the ship sank and everyone on board was drowned.

Whether this story is fact or fiction is not certain. It was an old story even at the time of Cicero. Nonetheless, it contains elements that have continued to appear in dreams on down through the centuries.

Rose Anne K. experienced a modern version, in which a favorite uncle appeared in a lucid dream years after his passing in order to give her a warning:

I had always loved him best and missed him dearly. When he appeared to me in a dream I was beside myself with joy. It was so real, not like a dream but as though I were awake and in my living room. He told me he had something very important to say but very little time. "You must be very careful this year, you are in danger." I reached out my hand and touched his cheek. I could feel him and I ached to embrace him but he pulled away and walked out of the room.

He was right. I hesitate to elaborate, but suffice it to say vigilance made the difference.

6

Unfinished Business

In 1321, the great Italian poet Dante Alighieri died of malaria. He had just completed the final portion of his masterpiece, *Divine Comedy*, a work on which he had labored for 13 years. The three-part work described his guided journey through Hell (Inferno), Purgatory (Purgatorio) and Heaven (Paradiso). There was, however, a problem: no one knew where he had stored the final pages of Paradiso. Without them, the work was incomplete.

Dante's sons searched in vain for the manuscript pages. A breakthrough came when son Pietro had a dream in which his dead father appeared and told him where to find the pages. They were hidden behind a mat hanging on a wall in a house where Dante had once lived. Pietro wasted no time in following his father's instructions, praying that he would not be too late. He was not. Pietro retrieved the missing pages, and the rest is literary history.

Dreams visits from the dead to complete unfinished business have been recorded throughout history. Usually the dreams concern wills, estates, and legacies of all kinds, though any kind of unfinished business can be dealt with in dreams. People die every day with all kinds of tasks, projects and intentions left undone. They can no longer be present in the physical world to wrap them up—but they can enter the dreams of those who can finish the business for them.

Proper burial

All societies since ancient times have observed burial rites to send the dead on their way to the afterlife. Proper burial is vitally important to the living as well, for it offers closure.

The grateful dead

The dead pay attention to their burial as well, and if something is amiss, they appear in dreams and waking visions to say so. The concern of the dead over their burial is a universal motif in folklore, called the "grateful dead." The typical story is thus:

A hero starts out on a journey and comes upon a group of people who will not bury a man who died before paying his debts. Or, the group is abusing the man's corpse. The hero gallantly gives all his money to either pay the man's debts or pay for proper burial. He goes on his way. He is quickly joined by a mysterious companion (usually a human but sometimes an animal), who brings him great fortune, saves his life, helps him accomplish a seemingly impossible feat, finds a princess for him to marry, and so on. At the end of the story, the hero learns that the mystery companion is really the grateful dead person.

Wandering shades

The ancient Greeks believed that when a person died, they made a one-way journey to Hades, the underworld. The shades, as the souls of the dead were called, did not return to the living world except under certain circumstances. One of them was improper burial. In fact, improper burial meant that a shade could not enter Hades, but was forced to wander the earth in sadness and despair until burial rites were performed. In such cases, the dead were allowed to return to a living person in a dream and ask for burial.

The fate of the unburied and improperly buried was depicted in Homer's *Iliad*, written around the 8th century BCE. The warrior Patroclus was killed in battle in the Trojan War and, like many of the fallen, was not buried. Patroclus appeared to his comrade Achilles in a dream and asked for burial by rite of burning. He appeared wearing his battle armor, looking sad and unhappy, and "stood" over the head of Achilles as he slept. He said the souls of dead men prevented him from entering Hades. If Achilles would bury him, he would never again come back from the land of the dead.

Achilles reached out to touch Patroclus, who seemed so life-like, but he disappeared beneath the ground like vapor. All night long, Patroclus pleaded for burial. Achilles did as instructed, and organized a funeral pyre and rite to burn the corpse of Patroclus. With that, the dead warrior was at rest and peace.

Unhappy with grave

The Sefer Hasidim notes that many recurring dreams deal with questions of proper burial, such as in this account of a saintly dead person who was unhappy with his burial location, and appeared in mass dreams to complain about it:

> It happened that a saintly sage was buried next to one who was unworthy. The saint came to all the townspeople in a dream and said, "You did me evil in that you buried me next to a toilet that has a stench. The fumes are hard on me." They placed stones between the grave of the saint and the grave of the evil-doer as a divider; from that time on he [the saint] did not come to them in a dream.

The sage sent his dream to a group of people—the entire town. It is possible for more than one person to receive the same dream, or to have similar dreams at the same time.

An exposed casket

Protestation of improper burial is a recurring dream theme that cuts across all religious and time lines. Such dreams continue to occur in modern times, in which the dead communicate that they are not at peace because of something amiss with burial. Gary D. was told the following account by his father:

> In 1931, my father's brother, Earnest, went to work at a bakery with my grandfather. He got a bad stomach ache and my grandfather brought him home. When he got home, he was very sick to his stomach. My grandmother called the doctor, and he thought Earnest just had a bad stomach ache from something he ate at the bakery. The doctor suggested giving him Castor oil, a laxative. Over the next few hours, Earnest got worse and was rushed to the hospital. They determined his appendix had burst, but it was too late to save him. He died at 17 in 1931.
>
> My grandmother was heartbroken. Earnest's body was brought in a casket back to their home. Though my father was only about seven years old at the time, he remembered this vividly up until his death in 1995. In those days the undertakers actually came to the house to do the embalming. My father asked his father if he could watch. After the body was prepared, over the next few days they had the wake at the house. Then Earnest was brought to the cemetery and was buried. My grandmother cried for weeks after this.
>
> A casket is usually placed inside another wooden box for protection. This is usually done after the family leaves the cemetery, so my grandmother never saw this.
>
> Sometime after Earnest was buried, and during a dream, my grandmother claimed to have seen a corner of the box which was not covered. She continued to insist she saw this in her dream and was disturbed by it.
>
> Finally, my grandfather went back to the cemetery to put his own mind to rest. The earth had settled and a corner of the exterior wooden

box was indeed uncovered! My grandfather covered it, and I believe it was several years before he told my grandmother that her dream was fact.

Gary's uncle, Earnest, did not appear himself in this dream, but information not known to any of the family was revealed in it. After the coffin corner was covered up, the distress ended.

Money matters

Another important matter that brings the dead into dreams concerns disposal of their personal belongings, money and estates. The dead may appear in recurring dreams until the business is closed.

Donating clothing

An account from the Middle Ages tells about a dead canon who came to a colleague in a dream to complain about his effects being kept. It had been the canon's policy to donate clothing of the dead to the poor. The next day, the colleague had the canon's cape given to beggar. That night, the canon appeared in a dream again, dressed in the cape. Apparently he was pleased, as he never returned in a dream again.

Settling debts

Unpaid debts may trouble the dead, who return to ask the living to settle their account. Anne Simpson was a Scotswoman in the early 19th century who casually knew a woman by the last name of Maloy, who died. Suddenly, Simpson began having dreams in which the dead woman urged her to see a priest, who would pay a small sum of money that she owed to another person, who was not identified in the dream. At first Simpson ignored the dreams, but they occurred nightly. Finally, greatly agitated, she sought out a priest and told her story.

The priest investigated and verified that a woman named Maloy had indeed died. She had worked as a washerwoman. He made further inquiries and found a grocer who acknowledged that Maloy owed him exactly the sum of money the dead woman had told Simpson in her dreams. The priest paid the debt. Simpson had no more dreams of the washerwoman.

The case is an example of how dream messages from the afterlife find a recipient, like electricity following the path of least resistance. Simpson barely knew the dead woman, but perhaps her unique characteristics of dreaming enabled Maloy to get through. We have no way of knowing whether Maloy had attempted to send a message to someone she knew better.

Settling estates

When people die unexpectedly, their survivors may not know where all their important papers and information are stored, such as financial accounts and wills. Like Dante revealing his missing manuscript pages, the dead may return to tell the living where to look. Bonnie McEneaney, whose husband Eamon died in the World Trade Center attacks (mentioned earlier in this book), collected dreams and other visitation experiences of 9/11 survivors and others as well:

> One of my neighbors… told me that after his father died, he was unable to locate some papers that were important to the estate. He had just about given up his search when he had a dream in which his father came and gave him precise instructions on where to locate the missing documents.

An unusual case of dreams that changed a will took place in the 1920s in North Carolina. The Chaffin Will Case was studied by psychical researchers who considered a range of explanations for the return of the dead man in dreams. The only explanation that holds up is an actual visit from the afterlife to set affairs straight.

James L. Chaffin was a farmer in North Carolina who had four sons. In November 1905, he made out a will leaving his farm and all assets to his third son, Marshall. He made no provision for his wife and three other sons, John, James P. and Abner.

Apparently Chaffin later had a change of heart, perhaps after reading the Bible. Genesis 27 tells how Jacob deceived his father, Isaac, into giving him the birthright intended for his older brother, Esau. In 1919, Chaffin executed a second will, written in his own hand, stating:

> After reading the 27th Chapter of Genesis, I, James L. Chaffin, do make my last will and testament, and here it is. I want, after giving my body a decent burial, my little property to be equally divided between my four children, if they are living at my death, both personal and real estate, divided equal if not living, give share to their children. And if she is living, you must all take care of your mammy. Now this is my last will and testament. Witness my hand and seal.
>
> James L. Chaffin
> This January 16, 1919

Though not witnessed, the will was valid under North Carolina law.

Chaffin then took the will and hid it in his father's old Bible. He secreted it in Genesis 27, folding pages to form a pocket to hold the paper. For reasons unknown, he said nothing to anyone of his new will. It is possible that he intended to do so at an appropriate moment, but was unable to follow through. However, Chaffin did write a note, "Read the 27th Chapter of Genesis in my daddie's old Bible," which he rolled up, tied with string and placed in the inside pocket of his black overcoat. He stitched the pocket shut.

On September 7, 1921, Chaffin died of injuries sustained in a fall. His 1905 will was probated, and the entire estate went to Marshall Chaffin. No one contested.

Four years later, in 1925, son James P. Chaffin began having vivid dreams in which his father appeared at his bedside and stood in silence. In June 1925, the deceased Chaffin appeared by his bedside once again, dressed in his black overcoat. He took hold of his coat, pulled it back and said, "You will find my will in my overcoat pocket." He vanished.

It is not certain whether the final appearance of the father was an external apparition or was part of a dream. James was not certain that he was awake or asleep when his father appeared; he may have been dozing.

The next morning, James awoke convinced that his father had communicated with him for the purpose of clearing up some terrible mistake. He went to his mother's house, where he found out that the overcoat was in the possession of his brother, John. On July 6, he visited John and found the coat. Upon examining it, James found the pocket that had been sewn shut. He opened it, found the note and read it.

James wisely found witnesses to accompany him back to his mother's to retrieve the Bible in question. They included Thomas Blackwelder, a neighbor, Blackwelder's daughter, and James's own daughter. They found the Bible and the new will.

The second will was filed in court and offered for probate. Marshall had died, but his widow and son contested the new will. The case came for trial in December 1925. About a week before the trial, the deceased Chaffin appeared again to James in a dream in an agitated state, saying, "Where is my old will." James took this to be a sign that he would win the lawsuit.

Ten witnesses were prepared to testify at the trial that the handwriting on the second will was that of the deceased Chaffin. When shown the will, Marshall's widow and son acknowledged that the handwriting was Chaffin's, and they withdrew their opposition. The old will was annulled and the new will was probated. Monies were redistributed, and Chaffin finally rested easy in the afterlife.

Several explanations were considered for this case:

1. James P. Chaffin, upset at being cut out of his father's will, forged a new and more favorable one and then concocted the dreams. However, the handwriting of Chaffin in the second will was validated as genuine. If son James P. Chaffin somehow did commit a forgery, there was no need for him to wait four years, or create a story that others would find hard to believe.

He could have simply "found" the new will, which would have been much more plausible.

2. The family of James P. Chaffin knew of the existence of the second will. However, a North Carolina attorney who was interested in parapsychology thoroughly interviewed James P. Chaffin, his wife, daughter and mother, and concluded that none of them had any prior knowledge of the second will. The lawyer said he was impressed with the Chaffins' honesty and sincerity.

3. James P. Chaffin had prior knowledge of the will, but had consciously forgotten it. The information may have been telepathically transmitted between father and son while the father was still living. The information was brought back to the son's attention by his dreams. This is possible, but not likely, given the known facts concerning the case. It is doubtful that the father revealed the new will to anyone; otherwise, he would not have gone to such great lengths to hide it. The four-year lapse also cannot be adequately accounted for by this theory.

4. During sleep, James P., through clairvoyance, obtained knowledge of the will, which was then projected into a dream and an "apparition" to present a plausible story and persuade himself that the information was true. This explanation cannot be ruled out, since the reaches of clairvoyance are unknown.

5. A genuine visit by the dead delivered information to James P. that was unknown to him. This theory supports survival after death. The four-year lapse gives added strength to the theory that the case is a genuine example of survival.

From the perspective of parapsychology, the case remains inconclusive, as none of these theories can be proved. However, people who have vivid visits from the dead in dreams know that the experiences are real, not imaginary.

The Chaffin Will case resembles a similar case that occurred near Ionia, Iowa in 1891. That case, too, involved a farmer, Michael Conley, who was found dead in an outhouse. Upon hearing of his death, Conley's daughter fell into a faint. Upon reviving, she said he had appeared to her and told her there was a large sum of money sewn inside a pocket inside the shirt he was wearing at the time of his death. She also described in detail his burial suit, including satin slippers that were of a new design, and which she could not have seen before. The clothes Conley had been wearing at the time of his death had been thrown away. They were recovered, and 35 dollars were found sewn shut in an inside shirt pocket.

Making amends

In various forms of communications, the dead describe going through a life review of their good points, bad points, successes, failures and so on. They stress that they are not held up to judgment by a supreme being who assigns them to eternal reward or eternal punishment, but rather they themselves are their harshest judge. They have spiritual help in determining how they need to improve, for the soul's work continues in the afterlife.

Sometimes the dead send a message to the living to apologize for something, usually a matter of importance to them and the person to whom they direct the message.

A mother's apology

Rhonda's mother was a difficult woman who spent much of her life grappling with emotional and physical problems. She died when Rhonda was 13. Rhonda's father sent her away to live with an aunt and uncle. Years later, when Rhonda was well into adulthood, she still harbored bad feelings and resentment about her early life.

Rhonda's brother remarried. One night the sister-in-law had a dream in which a woman kept repeating, "Tell her Mother's sorry, tell her Mother's sorry." She had never met her mother-in-law, who died before the marriage, but she had seen photographs, and thought the woman in the dream might be her. When she relayed the dream to Rhonda, asking if it made sense to her, Rhonda broke into tears.

In an interesting twist, Rhonda also said that when she had been sent to live with her aunt and uncle, she and a cousin got out a Ouija board one day and played with it. The board said there was a message for Rhonda. Then the board "went wild," spelling out "Mother's sorry, Mother's sorry."

Pop's regret

Erik's father was an alcoholic whose life was a roller coaster of unreliability. When he died at age 68, he and Erik had been estranged for much Erik's adult life. Upon hearing of his death, Erik was not even certain how he should feel. He said:

> There were so many broken promises and birthdays and holidays messed up that part of me just shut off and quit caring. Pop's drinking was hard on the entire family. He went through rehab twice but couldn't stay sober.
>
> About a week after the funeral, I was still in bad shape about it all. I felt like something had been stolen from me, first by the drinking and then by Pop's dying. I guess in the back of my mind I always had the hope that someday things would be "normal."
>
> This was really on my mind one night when I went to sleep. I'd been having trouble falling asleep, but this time I went straight into a very deep sleep. I must have been worn out.
>
> I had a dream that was so sharp and realistic that when I woke up, it was hard to think of it as a dream. I was sitting in a bare room that had only a table and two chairs. There was an old fashioned telephone on the table. Everything was gray—it reminded me of the interrogation rooms you see on TV shows.
>
> I sat there and then the phone rang. I picked it up and there was a lot of static. Then I heard Pop's voice. He said, "I'm sorry. I love you. I'm okay." Then the line went dead and I woke up.
>
> Pop had said he was sorry a lot when I was growing up, but it never

meant anything. I can' describe the emotion of this. It was like, silly as it sounds, his heart and soul were in it. I was deeply touched, like everything was all right. After I woke up, I said a prayer for him and thanked him and hoped he was at peace. It must have taken a lot of effort for him to contact me.

The bare, featureless room is a portrayal of the between places where meetings with the dead take place. A telephone, a symbol of long-distance communication, is another interesting element. The communication was short, as many afterlife messages are, but carried a powerful effect.

Incomplete projects and activities

In death, the concerns of daily life are released. Plans go unfinished, calendars are unfulfilled. In some cases, unfinished work is so important that the dead retain an energetic link to it and a desire to see it through somehow. They may appear in a dream with a request or instructions.

Two months after a young Belgian woman named Felicite died, her uncle-in-law had a vivid dream about her:

> It seemed to me that she entered the room where I lay asleep, and, sitting down on the bedside, asked me, as a favor, to look into an old tin box under the staircase for a certain wax candle, which had already been lighted, and which she had promised to Our Lady. On my consenting to do so, she took leave of me, saying, "Till the other world." I awoke from the dream much impressed. It was still dark, but I could no longer sleep.

A search revealed the tin box beneath the staircase. The candle—a kind used for prayers to saints and the Virgin Mary—was at the bottom. The wick had already been burned. The candle was taken to the local priest so that it could be lit again in Felicite's unfinished religious devotion, expressed from beyond the grave.

Avenging crimes and wrongful deaths

People whose deaths have not been solved or avenged may return in dreams to guide the living to the truth. Would a dead person's testimony stand up in court? In a strange case from the 19th century, dream evidence was introduced in a murder trial and played a role in a conviction.

The victim was a young woman named Elva Zona Heaster Shue, found mysteriously dead one day in 1897 in her West Virginia home. Her accused killer was her husband, Trout Shue, who bragged even after his arrest that there was no proof against him. He didn't bargain on revenge from the afterlife.

The story of Zona Shue, known as "The Greenbrier Ghost," is the only known case in the United States in which a dead person helped to convict a murderer by communicating from the afterlife. The case features three motifs prominent in folklore: the inability of a murder victim to rest until the truth is known; the return of the dead for revenge; and the disturbance of a sleeping person by a visit from the dead.

Little is known about the life of Zona. Born in the 1870s, she lived an ordinary life in a tiny community in Greenbrier County. In 1895, she had an illegitimate child.

In 1896, Zona met Edward (or Erasmus) Stribbling Trout Shue, a handsome stranger who arrived to work as a blacksmith in town. Within a few weeks, Trout and Zona were married, much to the disapproval of Zona's mother, Mary Jane Robinson Heaster, who took a strong dislike to Trout.

Mary Jane had good reason to disapprove. Shue had a dazzling personality and completely beguiled Zona, but he had a checkered past as a bully and wife beater. His first wife ran away to escape his abuse. His second wife, who was only 15, died under mysterious circumstances.

The marriage between Zona and Trout lasted about three months. In early January 1897, Zona fell ill and was under a doctor's care. On January 23, 1897, Shue had an 11-year-old black boy call upon Zona to see if she needed anything while Shue was out working. When the boy arrived at the Shue home, he discovered Zona's body lying on the floor. Her head was inclined slightly to one side.

Shue and the doctor were summoned. By the time Dr. George Knapp arrived, Shue had already carried his wife's body upstairs and, strangely, dressed it up in her Sunday best: a dress with a high neck and stiff collar secured by a big bow, and a veil covering her face. While Knapp attempted to determine the cause of death, Shue remained planted by his wife's head, cradling her head and upper body and sobbing in great distress.

Because of Shue's tremendous display of grief, Knapp made only a cursory examination. He observed slight discolorations on the right side of Zona's neck and right cheek. When he tried to examine the back of her neck, Shue erupted into such protests that Knapp ended the examination and left. He recorded the cause of death as "childbirth," a catch-all explanation for women.

Shue continued to behave oddly throughout the wake and funeral. He stayed close to the body at all times and would let no one, not even her mother, near it. He wailed and cried. People noticed that Zona's head seemed unusually wobbly and had to be propped straight with pillows and wads of cloth. A huge scarf was tied around her neck. Tongues wagged. Heaster was certain her daughter had not died an accidental death.

After Zona's burial, Heaster prayed that her daughter would come back from the dead and reveal the truth about how she died. She suspected the blacksmith of murder.

Heaster's prayers were answered within days. On four nights, Zona appeared and awakened her from sleep, or, appeared in dreams in which Heaster felt awake. Zona was dressed in the dress she had died in, and appeared solid, like flesh and blood. When Heaster reached out her hand, Zona disappeared. The next night, Zona appeared again and talked to her mother.

On the third night, Zona came again, and on the fourth night Zona described in detail her murder. Her husband had been abusive and cruel, she said. He had attacked her in a fit of rage because he thought she had no meat cooked for supper. He grabbed her head and broke her neck. To illustrate, Zona's head turned completely around on the neck.

Heaster went to the prosecutor, John Alfred Preston, who ordered Zona's body exhumed. Shue vigorously opposed the inquest. He publicly said that he knew he would be arrested, "but they will not be able to prove I did it," thus indicating he knew that his wife had been murdered. Zona's body was exhumed on February 22, 1897. An autopsy revealed a broken neck and a crushed windpipe from strangulation. There was no evidence of violence to other parts of her body. Shue was arrested and charged with first degree murder. He pleaded not guilty.

In jail, Shue remained in good spirits, his grieving gone. He bragged that he wanted to have seven wives, and since Zona was his third and he was only 35, he stood a good chance of realizing his ambition. He said repeatedly that his guilt could not be proved. He wondered why no one suspected the black boy as the killer.

All the evidence against Shue was circumstantial; it is doubtful the case would have ever been tried in modern times. Nonetheless, the trial commenced in late June 1897 in district court and lasted for eight days. Numerous people testified against Shue.

Heaster's story was hearsay, but the defense raised it when she was on the stand, perhaps in an effort to make her appear unbalanced and insane. Heaster recounted Zona's assertion that Zona's neck had been "squeezed off at the first vertebrae" by Shue.

According to Heaster, Zona's visits were not really dreams, but visions she had while awake. The defense attempted to get her to say they were dreams founded on her "distressed condition of mind," perhaps so Biblical injunctions against dreams could also be invoked. Heaster stuck to her story and its details. She also stated that Zona described the house where she and Shue had lived, a place Heaster had never seen or visited. The details were accurate.

With Heaster's story entered into the trial by the defense, the judge could not instruct the jury to disregard it. Most people in town had already heard the story, anyway, and believed it.

Shue's testimony was not cohesive and he rattled on about unimportant events, but he passionately denied everything said about his alleged guilt. It was to no avail. The jury returned a guilty verdict. Two of the jurors would not agree to a death sentence, and so Shue was sentenced to life in prison. After three years behind bars, he died, probably of an epidemic. There is no record of what happened to his remains.

Did Mary Jane Heaster fabricate the visits by Zona in order to implicate Shue? Had it not been for her story, the body probably never would have been exhumed, and Shue would have skipped town a free man. We may never know what really happened; however, Heaster's experiences are comparable to other dreams visits by the avenging dead.

How to handle unfinished business dreams

Treat dream messages about unfinished business as serious matters. As can be seen in the above examples, the living do not always have knowledge of the situations, and may even doubt whether the dreams have any meaning at all.

Sometimes the matter can be resolved within the dream itself or in prayer later, such as assuring the dead that it is all right to let go of daily affairs that are now left behind. In other cases, especially involving dreams that are urgent and repeating, investigate ways to help bring unfinished business to closure.

7

Helping the Dead

Many cross-cultural beliefs about the dead hold that they naturally linger on the earth plane for a while after their passing. They may remain close to their body until burial and can be sensed at home and other places. Then they move on. The living can help the dead by not encouraging them to stay. Our wakes, memorial services, burial rituals and prayers aid the transition for both the dead and the living, closing one door so that another can open.

Sometimes the dead do not move on. They appear in our dreams because they need our help to make a complete transition—they need "post-death releasement." They may have difficulty letting go of something left behind, such as unfinished business. They may be confused about where they are or feel temporarily stuck. If they died unexpectedly, they may wake up in an unfamiliar "body" and wander about trying to get the attention of the living. Or, they may be in a state of rest and healing, and need the balm of prayers. In all these cases and others, prayer for the dead is the most powerful aid we can give them. Mediums and psychics who are skilled in releasement can help souls find the light of the afterlife. Dreams, too, are instrumental.

Crossings

I had a post-death releasement dream after the death of my father, who was upset about unfinished business and was delaying his transition. I had always been close to him, and was devastated when he died of a ruptured aneurysm. At the time of his passing, he was active in his passion, amateur astronomy. His calendar was filled with upcoming events.

Eighteen months prior to death, Dad suffered a burst abdominal aneurysm and was rushed to the hospital. Doctors said he would not survive the emergency surgery, but he did. He was diagnosed with a second aneurysm threat in his chest, one that was inoperable due to its location and his weakened condition.

Dad resumed as much of his activities as he could, although he was in chronic pain. Eventually he suffered the second aneurysm, and died on the operating table. I had the feeling that Dad felt somewhat cheated: he had struggled through a painful recovery, only to have life snatched away.

About two weeks after his death, I had this intense and realistic dream meeting with him:

I am at my parents' house, sitting in a chair in the living room. Mom is home, somewhere in the house, but I do not see her; I just know she is there. Across from me, sitting in his favorite easy chair, is Dad. I know he's dead, and he knows he's dead, and that I know it, too. I also know that I am the only one who can see him. The room is lit with a peculiar bright light, and there is strange electricity in the air. I feel rather strange.

I say, "Dad, what are you doing here? You're dead! You can't stay here. You've got to move on."

Dad smiles and shakes his head. He explains to me that he has things he still has to do here. I argue with him: He's dead and he must not stay.

The scene suddenly shifts. I am no longer in my parents' house, but am watching Dad disappear into the distance. He is walking into a large building. Somehow I know it is a factory, or something like it—a place where work is done. Dad is going to work.

I had no doubt that I'd had a real encounter with my father, and that it concerned his need to fully leave the earth plane. Upon awakening, I could not recall the exact content of our conversation, but it had seemed to be quite detailed, and our meeting had the feeling of lasting a long time. In life, Dad could be stubborn. I could well imagine his irritation that death inconveniently interrupted his upcoming plans and activities. The symbolism of being in the living room of the house was not lost on me.

Evidently I prevailed upon Dad, since the next dream scene was one of transition. Dad going "to work" in a "factory" seemed apt symbolism. Throughout his life, Dad was a continual student, interested in learning about many things, especially the nature of the cosmos. Astronomy provided many hours of pleasure to him. He had projects going all the time, making things, building things, investigating things. He was recognized in amateur astronomy, with an observatory named after him: The Pettinger-Guiley Observatory in Puyallup, Washington, operated by the Tacoma Astronomical Society. I knew that in the afterlife, Dad would not be one to prop his feet up, but would want to plunge into a new line of work.

I did not have the feeling that Dad was stuck and unable to move on himself. Rather, he needed a nudge, and the dream happened in order to provide the opportunity for one. Interestingly, my mother, who had quite a bit of psychic ability, told me that she had felt Dad's strong presence in the house for about two weeks after his death. He often sat in his favorite easy chair in the living room. Then suddenly the energy was gone, and she knew he had made a complete transition to the afterlife. She had no knowledge of my dream when she told me about her impressions.

A confused sister

After the death of his sister, Richard L. had a dream in which he realized that she did not know she was dead, and was wandering in confusion. Here is his story:

Susan, my oldest and closest sister, was on her way to visit us in California. She had gotten herself into a marriage that she wanted to get out of for many reasons. She and her husband and one boy about 14 years old were on their way from the state of Washington to our home in California. A station wagon crossed a double median and struck their car head-on, instantly killing my sister, who was driving. The next few days were hell for me and our family.

Approximately three months later the following either occurred or I dreamed it:

I had gone to bed around 10:30 PM. Sometime during the night I found myself lying on a brown couch. I sat up and looked around. There didn't seem to be any ground, just fluffy clouds. As I looked off into the distance, a figure seemed to be approaching. It was dressed in a brown burlap-type robe with a hood on it. No matter how close it came I couldn't see a face inside the hood, just a black space.

The figure stopped a little distance from me and asked, "What are you doing here?"

I answered, "I am here to help my sister across. She doesn't know she is dead."

"What makes you think you can help her," it asked.

I answered, "My grandfather is waiting and he will help me show her the way across." The figure turned and walked away.

Next I saw another figure approaching. It was my sister. She was mumbling, "It's so cold, where is everyone? Why won't somebody help me?" As she approached she left footprints in the cloud-like stuff. I called to her but she didn't seem to hear me, but continued towards me.

When she came within reach I took her hand. She looked at me but didn't seem to see me. All she said was, "I'm so cold and you're so warm."

I started walking, holding her hand as she kept mumbling the same words. In the distance ahead I could see what seemed to be a bridge. I led her to the bridge. Standing on the other side were my grandfather and grandmother. They didn't seem to see me, but they stretched out their hands and called my sister to come to them. Susan recognized them, let go of my hand and crossed to their arms.

I awoke the next morning feeling wonderful knowing that at last my sister had crossed to where our people were waiting and she could be at peace.

Richard's experience indicates that Susan may have been confused by her sudden and unexpected death, and thus was unable to move on. Such circumstances can lead to a soul becoming earthbound until they receive help, or until they are able to find the path to the afterlife on their own.

Transition involves such symbolic events as walking into a brilliant light, going through a doorway, or—as did Susan—going across a bridge. The transition point marks the barrier between the worlds. When the living provide transition assistance in dreams, they know, or they are told by a voice or another figure, that they cannot follow the dead across. These "points of no return" also are found in many near-death experiences.

Adjusting to a new environment

Robert Monroe said he often helped the newly dead adjust to their new surroundings. Sometimes when he was out-of-body, he was called or drawn by a signal or energy that pulled him to another location, where he found another person in need of help. He met newly deceased souls who had arrived in the astral plane but were not aware that they were dead. He talked to them to help them get comfortable and oriented.

Anne Beckley is a lucid dreamer who has done extensive training in energy healing. During her training, she had many lucid dreams filled with spiritual instruction from guides in classes on the astral plane. Some of the lessons she learned pertain to afterlife dreams, as well as to a more fulfilled life:

> The instructors always gave the same message: "Trust yourself." A lot of these dreams involved instructions for healing techniques, being more aligned with my Guided Self, and thus being able to work better with the energy bodies. We also were taught how to telepathically communicate with people. We learned about the structure of the universe, what is the fundamental nature of reality.
>
> In some dreams I've been practicing a lot of flying. At first I could only get three or four feet off the ground. Then later I got 11 to 12 feet off, and then up to the tree tops. In one dream I saw the silver cord attached to my body. I saw myself lying on the couch while I was flying around. I was in a third awareness.
>
> I controlled where I went. You just have to think about where you want to be. You don't actually need flying, you just use your mind.

Anne's lucid OBE dreams were permeated with vivid colors. "The colors are not of this earth," she said. "The colors are lighted from within objects, radiating out." She added:

> There was always a lot of love in these dreams. Nobody was there to correct you, but to guide you. It was a supportive environment.
>
> There was a male person, a guide, who often showed up. His appearance was sometimes different, but his eyes were always the same, an otherworldly blue that I've never seen here on earth. They were deep and compassionate and saw right through me with unconditional love.

Once Anne felt a need for a spiritual assignment, and asked her Higher Self for one. Several weeks later, Anne was given her assignment in a dream trip to the astral plane where she met the dead:

I awoke to a landscape where I knew I was dreaming of sorts, but it was not the usual dreamscape I am familiar with. There was an ocean with haze, but the ground was not the usual solid consistency. I realized that I was on the astral plane where people cross over when they have died. It was a blue island.

I knew that I had not died, but at first I did not realize my purpose there, until I had ascertained that I was on the astral plane. Seeing people emerge from various parts of the landscape, I knew that they had just crossed over. Some did know where they were, but others, alas, had no idea where they were.

One man had drowned. I asked him if he knew where he was. He replied that he had been drowning, but was now saved and was just fine. I had to gently let him know that he was dead and had crossed over, but he was in total disbelief.

I asked him what was the last thing he remembered before coming here. He said he was drowning, but it was now obvious that he had been saved and was okay. I said that that was just the point, he had drowned, and since he was just fine he now found himself in a new land, the astral plane.

He was angry. I wanted to shout, "You're dead, get a grip, you cannot go back," but I acted with diplomacy in greeting the new folks arriving.

I was given a lit blue candle (an unreal blue not found on Earth) that had an inscription along the top wax which I could not decipher, by a gentleman who obviously was a teacher or guide. I knew I was supposed to give the welcome ritual, but I felt so unprepared, or rather unworthy, of this assignment. I took with courage this assignment, and greeted the new arrivals to the astral plane to explain where they were. Again, some others accepted this, and others were in shock and disbelief. I explained that there are new rules which govern existence, and over time everyone would be learning about the new environment, how to navigate and what lessons each person would learn over time. The island held an ocean, a bay, a marsh and a cornfield, with a small town with more of a populace.

I felt I was given my first assignment as a neophyte soul. My first lesson was to recognize where I am in the dreamscape; in this case it was the astral plane. My second lesson was to have compassion.

Anne's afterlife dream experiences had a dual purpose of helping the dead and helping her learn how to navigate the astral plane. In the case of the drowning victim, he was unwilling to accept his death. However, Anne's encounter with him was the first step in his acceptance process.

Rest and healing

Dreams sometimes alert us that the dead are in stages of rest and healing. The soul may need some time out, or may be adjusting after a long illness or a sudden and violent death. Within a year of her father's death, Cheryl Alsippi had this dream:

> I was standing inside a house, inside a sun room with all the windows around me (they were closed) and a sidewalk all around the outside of it. All of a sudden, my father walked into view outside the room (coming from the right, if this is significant). He continued to walk around the outside of the room and I started calling to him, yelling "Hey, old man...Hey" et cetera (I never called my father that in life). But, he never looked at me or acknowledged that he heard anything, just kept looking straight ahead and walked on.
>
> An even odder part of this story is that when Mitch Albom's book, *The Five People You Meet in Heaven* came out, I read it immediately. I was astonished when I came to a scene in the book where the main character was dreaming and in the dream was inside a diner. He saw a loved one who had passed on, walking around outside the diner. He kept calling to her, but got no response.
>
> Some years later when I was speaking with a psychic medium and brought up the possibility of getting information on my father, she told me that after he passed, he spent a lot of time (unknown amount) in a healing period due to life trauma before he moved on.

Cheryl's dream serves as an example of afterlife dreams that alert the living to the status of the dead. She was unable to communicate with her father. These dreams are like looking through windows. Their purpose may be to reconnect us emotionally, and especially to stimulate prayer. Prayer energy is healing and can quicken the restoration process on the Other Side. The dead are aided by spirit helpers, but they also govern their own adjustments to the afterlife.

How to use dreams to aid the dead

When dreams allow communication, a gentle conversation about the need to move on into the afterlife is beneficial. Even if there is no indication of resolution within the dream, a helpful process is started.

When there is no "reckoning" conversation, pray for the dead and visualize them moving into a new life of restored energy, peace, love and happiness. Invoke the help of spiritual figures to come to their aid.

8

Animals in the Afterlife

Inky, a sleek black cat with a bold white chest, died one night in the arms of her owner, Chris DeChello. Like most pet owners, Chris had a deep emotional bond with Inky and greatly grieved her passing:

> She died in the best place she wanted to be, and vice-versa. Inky was my constant companion, and as a kitten, she entertained me through my cancer treatments. That was 20 years ago, and I feel that she lived a long and happy life.

Within a day or so, Inky was back for a reassurance visit. Said Chris:

> I saw one flash of Inky yesterday. I sometimes have sightings of well-loved pets that have already crossed the rainbow bridge. I call these visits a gift. I am sure that I will get more visits from her in the future. Inky was my heart and soul.

Animals have souls, and they do go into an afterlife. They go to the same place as humans, where they can reunite with their human loved ones.

Many people who have lost a beloved pet are visited by their pet in both dreams and in waking consciousness. The return visit is taken as a sign of a loving bond that continues after death. People may hear, smell or see their pet, and even feel a physical but invisible presence. The visits are usually very comforting, and can help ease a person's grief.

Dog dreams

After my two dogs, Tessie and Honey Dog, passed away, I had vivid dreams of them. They were mother (Tessie) and daughter (Honey Dog). I have had a number of pets throughout my life and have cherished them all, but I was especially close to these two dogs. Nearly every day, I took them for runs in the countryside. They loved to be off leash and run through the woods and fields as fast as they could.

Honey Dog died first, of cancer. She passed away at home, at a time of her own choosing. Tessie did not last much longer. She developed kidney and bladder issues, and we had to make the difficult decision to send her to rest. It was the hardest thing I have ever had to do in my life.

My dreams of them were vivid and lucid, and felt like the real-time present. We were often out on the walks. I could feel the breeze and smell the woods. I also felt the joy they felt at running, in the peaks of their lives. I always had the feeling that wherever they were, they were really enjoying themselves. I know I will see them again, as well as my other pets, too.

Many animal return visits are manifestations of their presence in their old home.

An invisible presence

Joshua P. Warren is a paranormal researcher in North Carolina. When his miniature dachshund, Nellie, died, she came back for a while. Joshua heard her familiar whimpers and barks in empty rooms in his house, and also heard the sounds of her little toenails on the hardwood floor. He did not see Nellie, but felt a strong sense of her presence on several occasions. Nellie's ghost remained for about a week and then faded away. Joshua tried to capture evidence of Nellie with photographic and recording equipment, but was not successful. However, he was firmly convinced from his own experiences that Nellie had in fact returned to visit him.

Experiences such as Joshua's have been reported by so many people that it is difficult to explain them away as imagination or wishful thinking as a result of sorrow and grief.

Characteristics of animal returns

Visits by pets fall into certain patterns. They usually make themselves known soon after death, and for a short period of time, such as a few days or a week or two. They behave as they did when they were alive. For example, a deceased cat may be glimpsed as it jumps up on a sofa or bed. The weight and feel of an animal may be experienced as well, such as the shape of their body and the texture of their fur. A bird may be heard chirping in the room where it was kept. Often, the animals are not seen, but are heard, smelled and sensed.

As time passes, the strength of their presence diminishes until it stops altogether. Sometimes, people report that their dead pets return for visits occasionally for years. A small number of pet owners say they feel a constant presence of their departed pets.

Not all pets return, just as all deceased people do not return for visits.

Realistic dreams of pets share the characteristics of dreams of departed people: lucidity, vivid colors, a "strange" feel to the environment. However, the settings are usually earth or earth-like: pets at home, and pets at play in favorite places.

Animal communicators

Many people seek out the help of mediums known as animal communicators to make contact with their deceased pets. Animal communicators are able to converse with all kinds of animals, and they convey messages to the humans left behind.

Animals even give helpful advice. In Kim Sheridan's book *Animals and the Afterlife: True Stories of Our Best Friends' Journey Beyond Death*, animal communicator Sharon Callaghan had a case in which a deceased cat, Wiggie, told her owner that her apartment was a "toxic place." The owner later found out that her paint contained asbestos.

Animals in spirit communications

Animals understand and learn words and verbal and hand commands. They also communicate on a much more subtle level. Every pet owner knows how to exchange thoughts with their pets. All I had to do was think the word "walk" and Tessie and Honey Dog would get excited. We often took them in the car with us, which they also enjoyed—but they always knew when they were going to the kennel or to see the vet, even if the words were never spoken.

The telepathic bond between people and animals has been studied scientifically by Rupert Sheldrake, a parapsychologist and former biochemist and plant physiologist. In his book *Dogs That Know When Their Owners Are Coming Home*, he documents cases showing that people and their pets have an empathic bond that enables two-way telepathic communication. Sheldrake does not speculate on the afterlife. However, as we have seen how the emotional bond between people can bridge the afterlife, it is reasonable to think that a similar bridge can connect people and animals.

In *Talking to the Dead*, which I co-authored with George Noory, the host of *Coast to Coast AM*, we feature evidence collected by spirit communications researchers that documents contact with animals in the afterlife. Some of the contacts are audio transmissions called Electronic Voice Phenomena (EVP), a term applied to audio communications from unknown origins:

In the 1980s, German researcher Klaus Schreiber reported that he captured an Electronic Voice Phenomena audio recording of a voice identifying itself as Jakob, his deceased pet crow. Since 1998, Anabela Cardoso, researcher and editor of Instrumental Communication Journal, has received several direct radio voice communications from Nisha, one of her Doberman pinschers who resides on the Other Side.

Cardoso has reported other deceased animals who communicate in voice. For example, Brazilian researcher Sonia Rinaldi recorded a parrot, Lorinho, the former pet of her colleague Claudio Brasil. The parrot delivered a message in Portuguese.

Other contacts have included animal sounds recognizable to former owners.

A dying dog sends a farewell dream

Most afterlife contacts with pets are return and reassurance visits. It is possible for animals to make farewell visits as they die. One of the most unusual cases on record was documented by psychical researchers Edmund Gurney, F.W.H. Myers and Frank Podmore in *Phantasms of the Living*. The case concerned a dying dog who appeared in a farewell visit dream. It took place in England in 1904, and was first reported in *The Times* on July 21. The experiencer was a man named Rider Haggard, whose oldest daughter owned a black retriever named Bob. The Haggards lived in Ditchingham, Norfolk, on the River Waveny, across from Bungay, Suffolk.

According to Haggard, on the evening of July 9, he retired to bed about 12:30 and suffered a nightmare. He was awakened by his wife, who heard him making strange sounds. Haggard said:

All I could remember of it was a sense of awful oppression and of desperate and terrified struggling for life such as the act of drowning would probably involve. But between the time that I heard my wife's voice and the time that my consciousness answered to it, or so it seemed to me, I had another dream. I dreamed that... Bob... was lying on its side among brushwood, or rough growth of some sort, by water. My own personality in some mysterious way seemed to me to be arising from the body of the dog, which I knew quite surely to be Bob and no other, so much so that my head was against its head, which was lifted up at an unnatural angle. In my vision the dog was trying to speak to me in words, and, failing, transmitted to my mind in an undefined fashion the knowledge that it was dying. Then everything vanished, and I woke up to hear my wife asking me why on earth I was making those horrible and weird noises. I replied that I had a nightmare about a fearful struggle, and that I had dreamed that old Bob was in a dreadful way, and was trying to talk to me and tell me about it.

Haggard went back to sleep. In the morning, the family discussed the dream. Mrs. Haggard stated:

> ...I was awakened by most distressing sounds proceeding from my husband, resembling the moans of an animal, no distinct words. After listening for a few moments, I woke him up, whereupon he said he had a nightmare, in which he was engaged in some struggle connected with our retriever dog "Bob," and that "Bob" was trying to talk to him and explain that he wanted help. It was quite dark at the time, so I concluded it must have been about 2 a.m.

The Haggards' daughter was present at breakfast, but thought surely the dog was fine, as she had last seen it at about 8 PM on Saturday night when she fed it. The family laughed off the dream.

Bob did not show up for either his breakfast or his supper on Sunday, however, and the family decided the dog was missing and possibly lost.

Haggard and a servant set out to search for Bob. On Thursday, July 14, they found his body floating in the Waveny River against a weir (a low dam) by the Falcony Bridge. The next day, Haggard was hailed by two plate-layers working on the Bungay road. They told him that the dog had been killed by a train. They took Haggard to the open-work bridge that crossed the river between Ditchingham and Bungay, where they had found some of Bob's remains early on Monday, July 11. The remains included a torn collar, which Haggard later identified as Bob's; coagulated blood, and bits of flesh on the train rails. Haggard found bits of black hair.

The men told Haggard that they saw the body of the dog later in the day, and that it floated down the river toward the weir. They believed that Bob had been struck by the last train that departed Ditchingham Saturday night at 10:25 PM. It would have reached the bridge at 10:27 PM.

Bob's body was examined by a veterinarian who said that his injuries— a shattered head and broken forelegs—were consistent with an impact by a train. Blood stains on the piles of the bridge indicated that Bob was knocked into the river. Haggard said the dog had probably gone hunting rabbits, which it liked to do at night, and perhaps paused to rest on the bridge.

The veterinarian said Bob most likely was killed instantly upon being hit, but Haggard could not dismiss the sensations of drowning, which were conveyed to him in the dream. He said:

> …I am absolutely convinced that when I had my dream the dog had been dead for at least three hours. Further, this appears to be evident: the injuries to the dog's head were such that death must have been instantaneous; and even though life lingered in the tissues, as a doctor to whom I was talking this morning told me it might do for a little while, from the moment that engine struck the dog's head, it must have been utterly incapable of thought or volition as we understand it—that is, its brain was destroyed; it was physically dead. It seems therefore that in order to produce the long subsequent impressions upon myself, it must have been

spiritually alive. In short, even supposing that I received those impressions at the moment of the death of the dog and stored them up for future use, or that those impressions were flying about in the air like a wheeling hawk waiting for an opportunity to settle on my head, they must still have been emitted by the personality of an animal that was already dead, doubly dead from the fatal injury followed instantly by drowning.

I seem therefore to come to this conclusion: either the whole thing is a mere coincidence and just means nothing more than indigestion and a nightmare, or it was the spirit of the dog on its passage to its own place or into another form, that moved my spirit, thereby causing this revelation, for it seems to be nothing less.

In a subsequent statement, Haggard added:

Bob, although he belonged to my daughter, who bought him three years ago, was a great friend of mine, but I cannot say that my soul was bound up in him.

He was a very intelligent animal, and generally accompanied me in my walks about the farm, and almost invariably came to say good morning to me. He was rather rheumatic, as he was getting into years—seven perhaps —but that did not prevent him from going after rabbits, generally in company with Bustle, my spaniel.

Haggard debated about reporting his dream at the risk of "ridicule and disbelief" but decided to do so for "scientific interest" and to use his real name. He was interviewed by both the media and psychical researchers, who collected corroborating accounts from all of the parties involved. He said he had never had any other telepathic dreams, though he had had accurate premonitions.

Like human farewells and reassurances, an emotional bond played a significant role in this experience. Haggard's daughter had a strong bond with Bob, too, but was not disturbed on the night of his death. Once again, the difference may be the way a person dreams.

9

Dreams That Foretell Death

When Jeri B. was 14, she had a dream that she automatically knew meant "bad news."

> In the dream, I was taking a math test. My teacher came to me and tapped my shoulder, telling me that someone was there to pick me up and I had to go home. I turned around to see my father at the door and I immediately started to cry because I knew he must have bad news. Then I woke up before I could find out what it was.
>
> A few days later I was taking a math test, and my teacher came up and tapped me on my shoulder. I started sobbing before I even turned around and then saw that my father was there. Apparently my great aunt and uncle had been robbed and killed at their store and my father had come to take me home.

Jeri discovered that this would not be the only foreshadowing of death to appear in her dreams:

Years later, my favorite aunt, who had been suffering with kidney failure, was on dialysis. She was also having problems with congestive heart failure, and there had been a couple of times that we had to rush to the emergency room when the doctors didn't think she was going to make it.

I had a dream where I was in a big round room with windows all around it. I couldn't see anything out the windows but clouds. My mother came in the room and said there was someone else there to see me and she left. Then I saw my grandmother come in and wave at me and left the room. My grandfather came in next. He was smiling and saying how great it was to be in heaven with his family, and he was especially happy now because he said my aunt would soon be joining them. I told him no, that I didn't want her to go, but he said it was her time. I woke up crying and couldn't forget about the dream.

A couple of weeks later I received a call saying I had to get to the hospital quickly. When I arrived it was too late. My aunt had already passed away.

There were more forewarning dreams as well. "All my life I have had dreams that connect me with relatives that have passed away and sometimes tell me of a death in the family to come," Jeri said. Not every relative who passes is announced in a dream, however. When the dreams do happen, Jeri knows that it is time for someone to make their transition, and that the passage cannot be stopped.

Forewarning dreams do not occur to everyone. Even when death is expected, such as in cases of terminal illness, these dreams can be unsettling —few people like to know when death is around the corner. Yet these dreams have their preparation and healing purpose, too.

Warnings of one's own death

Dreams that forewarn of a person of their own impending sudden death are unusual. We all know that someday we will die, but knowing the time and manner of our death is too much for many people to contemplate, and we have a natural shielding that prevents us from learning the specifics. In the past I have dealt with persons who were informed by psychics that they were going to die at a certain time and in a certain way (a very unethical thing to do), and as the "doom date" approached they suffered psychological breakdowns, the effects of which continued after the "doom date" had passed.

Prevailing wisdom in modern dreamwork holds that dreams have intrinsic healing power, and provide information as we are ready to comprehend and use it. Thus, forewarning dreams that do break through have a purpose of preparing a person who is ready for a transition and can cope with the knowledge.

Forewarning dreams may involve a preview of the fatal incident or moment; a message from the dead or their presence; visions of seeing one's self dead; or some other potent symbolism significant to the dreamer. (Note: Any dream involving one's own death or any of these features does not automatically foreshadow death, but could relate to aspects of one's life that are "dying," or coming to an end.)

9/11 premonition dreams

On September 11, 2001, 2,996 people died in the terrorist attacks that destroyed the World Trade Center in New York City. Afterward, thousands of reports were made about dreams that forecast this tragedy. People dreamed of planes flying into tall buildings, tall buildings crumbling to the ground, huge crowds of panicked people running in the streets, nuclear mushroom clouds over New York City, and great chaos and destruction. The majority of dreams contained elements of the disaster, but not the complete event, including the accurate date, time and place.

Some of those who died had premonitions about their impending deaths, and some of their family members did, too. They had no inkling exactly how, when or where, but that transition was going to happen soon.

Bonnie McEneary lost her husband Eamon in the attacks, as mentioned earlier in this book. Eamon worked for Cantor Fitzgerald on the 105th floor of the North Tower. Interestingly, he had survived the 1993 bombing of the World Trade Center, and had led about 60 people to safety. In the weeks approaching 9/11, however, he spoke often of his premonitions that the World Trade Center would be hit again, and that he was going to die soon. He urged family and friends to make the most of their time, because one never knows when a day will be the last.

In talking with other survivors, Bonnie learned of their premonitions, as well as post-death visits and messages. In her book, *Messages: Signs, Visits and Premonitions from Loved Ones Lost on 9/11*, she told about "Robert," who had a dream in the summer of 2001 in which he was in a building (but not the World Trade Center) and a jet crashed into it. He was very disturbed by the dream, and both he and his wife thought it quite strange and "weird."

In another case, the premonition dream was experienced by the wife of a victim, a Midwest man who was at the WTC on the fatal day to attend meetings. During the first week of September, Lorraine had an odd dream. She was looking at a line of people dressed in business clothing filing past her in slow motion. The people, and everything else, were in black, white and gray, no color. Suddenly she saw her husband, Bill, in the line and wondered what he was doing there. Then the man right behind Bill turned and looked at her. He had dark hair and was dressed in a dark topcoat, but was strikingly different from the others. He had intense dark, crystalline eyes and his teeth shone like neon lights. He was beautiful. He put his right hand up over Bill's head and pointed at him, whispering, "He's next."

Lorraine abruptly awakened, so shaken by the dream that she was in a cold sweat. The dream was so realistic that she expected to see the man standing in the bedroom.

No interpretation of the darkly dressed was offered in the description; however, it fits similar descriptions of Death and messengers of Death that have been recorded in dreams and waking visions. Death messengers are darkly dressed but often have an unearthly light around or about them. They may be frightening in countenance, but they are often beautiful. Many of the dead describe dying as a beautiful, easy experience.

Abraham Lincoln hears of his death

One of the most famous forewarning of death dreams occurred to President Abraham Lincoln. After seeing the nation through a difficult Civil War, Lincoln was assassinated on April 14, 1865 by John Wilkes Booth, an opponent of the abolition of slavery. Booth fatally shot the president at point black range in the back of his head as he watched a play at Ford's Theater with his wife, Mary Todd Lincoln. He died a few hours later.

Lincoln had startling premonitions of his own death that went beyond dreams. Shortly before his election to his first term in 1860, he saw a vision of himself in mirrors on several occasions that upset him. He would see two separate and distinct images of his face, one of which was deathly pale, and which vanished as he gazed at it. He told Mary about the faces, and she interpreted the vision as a sign that he would be reelected to a second term but would not survive it.

Ten days before his assassination, Lincoln had a dramatic dream of his own death. He wrote in his journal:

> I retired late. I soon began to dream. There seemed to be a deathlike stillness about me. Then I heard subdued sobs, as if a number of people were weeping. I thought I left my bed and wandered downstairs. There the silence was broken by the same pitiful sobbing, but the mourners were invisible. I went from room to room; no living person was in sight, but the same mournful sounds of distress met me as I passed along.

It was light in all the rooms; every object was familiar to me; but where were all the people who were grieving as if their hearts would break? I was puzzled and alarmed. What could be the meaning of all this? Determined to find the cause of a state of things so mysterious and so shocking, I kept on until I arrived at the East Room, which I entered. Before me was a catafalque, on which rested a corpse wrapped in funeral vestments. Around it were stationed soldiers who were acting as guards; and there was a throng of people, some gazing mournfully upon the corpse, whose face was covered, others weeping pitifully. "Who is dead in the White House?" I demanded of one of the soldiers. "The President," was his answer. "He was killed by an assassin." Then came a loud burst of grief from the crowd, which awoke me from my dream. I slept no more that night; and although it was only a dream, I have been strangely annoyed by it ever since.

The night before he was killed, Lincoln told a member of his cabinet that he had dreamed he would be assassinated. The day of his assassination, Lincoln confided to his bodyguard, W.H. Crook, that he a dreamed for three nights straight that he would be assassinated. Crook begged him not to go that night to Ford's Theater, but Lincoln said he had promised Mary that they would go. Perhaps he knew he would be shot that night, for when they departed for Ford's, Lincoln said "goodbye" to Crook instead of his customary "goodnight."

Meanwhile, a night-time premonition may have saved the life of General Ulysses S. Grant, who, with his wife, Julia, was to be with the Lincolns in the theater on the fatal night. Julia awoke that morning with an oppressive feeling that something terrible was going to happen. She persuaded Grant to stay home. Later, it was revealed that Booth planned to assassinate Grant as well that evening. It is not known if Julia had a dream, or awakened with a general sense of foreboding.

Lincoln's dreams were blunt and specific, and they repeated, which is a characteristic of many premonitory dreams that warn of an impending event. Few individuals would have the same calmness in facing their violent end. Why was Lincoln privy to his end via dreams when few others are? Lincoln may have had more than average psychic ability, as he had other paranormal experiences earlier in life. Both he and his wife had an interest in Spiritualism. Steering a divided nation required a strong psyche, and Lincoln may have felt that his end was a destiny that he had to fulfill.

The sun blots out

In the 12th century, King William II of England had an ominous dream that presaged his death. The dream did not directly foretell his demise, but it left the king feeling very uneasy about his life. In the dream, William was being bled. His blood spurted up so high into the air that the very sun was blotted out and day changed into night. The dream—more of a nightmare—awakened the king. He was so distressed that he called out to the Blessed Virgin Mary for assistance. He ordered his chamberlains to put on a light, and to stay with him. He did not go back to sleep.

The next day, August 2, 1100, the king set out hunting with several companions, among them a Frenchman named Walter Tirel, the Lord of Poix, who was a close friend of the king's. A chase of a stag began, and the hunting party scattered, except for Tirel and William, who remained together.

William shot an arrow into a stag wounded it. He had to shield his eyes against the sun to see where it ran. Another stag appeared and Tirel shot carelessly at it. He missed—but his arrow pierced the chest of the king by accident. Stunned, William pulled at the arrow, breaking the shaft. He then collapsed on top of the broken shaft, which drove it deeper into his body. He fell unconscious.

Tirel fled for his life, and the king expired. The rest of the hunting party soon came upon William's corpse. They did not pursue Tirel, but had to deal with the urgent matter of a successor. Local villagers had to load the king's body onto a cart for transport back to Winchester.

William's premonitory dream was recorded by the monk William of Malmesbury. It contained elements of the events to come—extreme bleeding, and even the sun being blocked out—and carried a heavy tone that distressed the king.

Caligula is rejected by the gods

One of the cruelest of Roman emperors, Caligula, had a dream the night before he was assassinated that warned of his impending death. Caligula, a nickname meaning "Little Boots" that he earned as a child in military camps, was born Gaius Julius Caesar Augustus Germanicus, and became emperor at age 23. He ruled from 37-41 CE. Even before taking the throne, he was known for excesses of sex and blood, and he quickly became despised as an oppressive ruler. Assassination plots against him were tried and failed, with the unlucky conspirators executed. Finally a plot succeeded that was aided by the Praetorian Guard, the soldiers who were supposed to guard him. When games were held at the Palatline Hill, it was Caligula's habit to leave early and exit through a secret underground passageway. He was ambushed there and stabbed to death.

The night before his murder, Caligula had a dream in which he stood before the throne of Jupiter, the ruler of the gods. Jupiter rejected him and kicked him back to earth. The symbolism would not be obvious to us today, but it portended ill for Caligula. From Augustus Caesar on, Roman emperors were regarded as gods-in-the-making who would join the pantheon of deities upon their death. For Caligula to stand in front of Jupiter, it meant his death—but the god rejected him, perhaps because of his atrocities.

The woman in white

The case of Lord Thomas Lyttleton, called the "Wicked Lord" and the "Bad Lord Lyttleton" because of his ill reputation, involves both a death warning apparition and a farewell visit. In 1779, Lyttleton returned from

Ireland to his house in Hill Street, Berkely Square, in London. He was visited by several guests, among them Lord Fortescue, Lady Flood, two unmarried sisters by the name of Amphlett, and a friend who recorded the account of Lyttleton's mysterious death at age 45. Lyttleton was not in good health, and had suffered suffocating fits during the preceding month. According to the account:

It happened that he dreamt, three days before his death, that he saw a fluttering bird, and that afterwards a Woman appeared to him in white apparel, and said to him, "Prepare to die; you will not exist three days."

His lordship was much alarmed, and called to a servant from a closet adjoining, who found him much agitated and in a profuse perspiration. The circumstance had a considerable effect all the next day on his lordship's spirits. On the third day, which was a Saturday, his lordship was at breakfast with the above personages [the guests], and was observed to have grown very thoughtful, but attempted to carry it off by the transparent ruse of accusing the others at the table of unusual gravity.

"Why do you look so grave?" he asked. "Are you thinking of the ghost? I am as well as ever I was in my life."

Later on he remarked, "If I live over tonight, I shall have jockeyed the ghost, for this is the third day."

The whole party presently set off for Pit Place [Lyttleton's gloomy mansion in Epsom, now a suburb of London], where they had not long arrived before his lordship was visited by one of his accustomed fits. After a short interval, he recovered, dined at five o'clock, and went to bed at eleven. When his servant was about to give him a dose of rhubarb and mint water, his lordship, perceiving him stirring it with a toothpick, called him a slovenly dog, and bid him go fetch a teaspoon.

On the man's return, he found his master in a fit, and, the pillow being placed high, his chin bore hard upon his neck; when the servant, instead of relieving his lordship on the instant from his perilous situation, ran, in his fright, and called out for help; but on his return he found his lordship dead.

Thus, the dream warning from the woman in white proved to be true. Since no identity of the woman is given in the account, she may have been a mysterious figure, a messenger from spirit. The bird is a symbol of spirit and the soul, and is associated with heaven.

Another apparition was connected to Lyttleton's death. On the day of his demise, Lyttleton and others planned to visit a nearby good friend of Lyttleton's, Miles Peter Andrews, Esq., who lived at Dartmoor. At the last moment, Lyttleton excused himself, perhaps because he was anxious about the death warning. He sent along no excuse to Andrews.

That night, Andrews went to bed early because he was not feeling well himself. Shortly after he retired (and perhaps was in a drowsy state), he was startled when the curtains of his four-poster bed were drawn aside by Lyttleton, who was dressed in one of his distinctive nightgowns. Andrews assumed that Lyttleton had decided to visit after all, and was playing a joke on him. He said to the figure, "You are up to some of your tricks. Go to bed, or I'll throw something at you."

Lyttleton merely gazed at him mournfully and responded, "It's all over for me, Andrews."

Andrews, still thinking his friend was playing a joke, picked up one of his slippers and threw it at Lyttleton, who then seemed to glide into the adjoining dressing room.

Angry, Andrews jumped up and searched both bedroom and dressing room, but found both empty, and the doors bolted from the inside. He rang his bell for his servants and asked them about Lyttleton, but the servants, puzzled, said he had not been in the house all evening. Andrews still did not suspect anything strange, and ordered the servants to deny Lyttleton a bed, saying he could instead go to one of the inns at Dartford.

The news of Lyttleton's death during the night reached Andrews the next day. He fainted when he heard it, and reportedly "was not his own man" for three years following.

There are variations in the story. In one, Andrews was invited to Pitt Place but declined because he was to be Dartmoor Mills, where he slept that night. Lyttleton died at midnight, and Andrews saw his apparition a few minutes after 12. Interestingly, the two had an after-death pact, in that the first one who died would try to contact the other.

Lyttleton's fits may have been seizures or strokes. His death would have been considered normal if not for the dream, which some said was the revenge of an allegedly evil deceased woman, Mrs. Amphlett, who was rumored to have died of a broken heart because Lyttleton had callously seduced both daughters.

Impending deaths of others

Sometimes dreams warn people of the impending deaths of others. There are ancient examples: In 44 BC, Calpurnia, the wife of Roman Emperor Julius Caesar, had a dream in which Roman senators stabbed a statue of her husband with knives, and blood flowed from the statue. Unbeknownst to her, several senators were indeed conspiring to kill the emperor. Calpurnia awakened certain that her husband would be killed that very day in public. She tried to warn Caesar, but he was skeptical. He relayed the dream to Decius, a senator who actually was among the assassination conspirators. Decius slyly interpreted the dream as a favorable omen of Rome's future victories under Caesar. Caesar went out as planned that day—and was stabbed to death by his enemies in front of the Theatre of Pompey.

Centuries later, another Roman emperor, Marcian (Flavius Marcianus) dreamed of the demise of his enemy, Attila the Hun, who died in 453 CE. The manner of Attila's death is uncertain, but he may have died by suffocating on his own blood from a bleeding nose. On the night of Attila's passing, Emperor Marcian stated he had had a dream whereby he saw Attila the Hun's bow break. In retrospect, the dream symbolized the breaking of Attila's military might against the Roman Empire, which would happen in the event of his death.

Previewing an assassination

In the early 20th century, two assassinations that helped to ignite World War I were previewed in a remarkable dream. Tensions were building in Europe, and by 1914 many people feared that war would erupt. On June 28, Bishop Joseph Lanyi of Grosswardein, Hungary, awakened from a nightmare that he knew would come true. Lanyi had once been the tutor of the Archduke Franz Ferdinand of Austria, one of the figures involved in the political tensions.

In the dream, Lanyi went to his desk to look through some letters. On top was a letter bearing the seal of the archduke; it was bordered in black like a death or funerary notice. Lanyi recognized the archduke's handwriting, and opened the letter. The top of it featured a postcard-like light blue picture of a street with a narrow passage. In a motorcar sat the archduke and his wife, a general who faced them, and the chauffeur and another officer. People were crowded on both sides of the street. The picture suddenly came to life in the dream with two young men leaping from the crowd and firing guns at the archduke and his wife. Below the picture was a note from the archduke, addressed personally to Lanyi. It read, "I hearwith inform you that today, my wife and I will fall victims to an assassination. We commend ourselves to your pious prayers." It was dated June 28, 3:45 AM, Sarajevo.

Layni awakened in tears at 3:45 AM. He immediately recorded the dream, sketched the scene, and had the drawing certified by two witnesses. He sent the account to his brother. He commenced earnest prayer.

The archduke and his wife were shot to death in their car almost as Lanyi had dreamed—there was one assassin, not two. Photographs published in the newspapers closely matched the scene Lanyi had seen in his dream.

Lanyi's dream was one of the most remarkable death forewarning dreams on record. Few dreams have such detail and accuracy. More common are feelings of forebodings, or knowledge that a certain person will die, but no details as to how, when or where.

Seeing someone in a casket

American author Mark Twain once had a vivid dream in which he saw his brother lying in a casket. His brother was not ill and in danger of dying, so Twain did not automatically assume the worst. Within a few days, however, he learned that his brother had died in an accident on a boat that suddenly exploded. When Twain went to the funeral, he was shocked to see his brother laid out in the casket exactly as he had seen in his dream.

In cases such as these, death is not anticipated. Individuals who receive death warning dreams about others usually have a strong emotional connection to the soon-to-be-departed: They are a family member, a close friend or associate, or have an emotionally intense relationship (such as the animosity that must have existed between Emperor Marcian and Attila the Hun). Even in those cases, dreaming of imminent death is still a severe trauma. By the time these dreams break through the veil, fate seems to be sealed.

Grandfather's warning

Visitation dreams have been part of Guy Lockhart's spiritual awareness from an early age. Born with a high degree of psychic sensitivity, he has a better understanding of the afterlife than many people. One dream in particular stands out—it forewarned of the deaths of his parents:

> I have had a connection with the spirit world from a very young age, and as loved ones have passed on it has become stronger and more prophetic in nature. I receive most visitations and experiences with the dead through my dreams, and one encounter in particular stands at the forefront of my mind. It was the summer of 2011 when I had come to live in my grandparents' home where I spent the majority of my childhood. My father had recently been released from the hospital after a bizarre and

difficult stay there, and the first night spent in the house came with a visitation from the spirit of my paternal grandfather. The experience was like lucid dreaming, as though my soul was awake and sitting up in the room, and my grandfather sat at the end of the couch looking at me. When I asked him why he had come he opened his mouth and blood poured down the front of his shirt. I woke up with feelings of foreboding and knowing that painful times were ahead.

Shortly after that visitation my mother was diagnosed with cancer. I had a gnawing feeling that she needed to go to the hospital as soon as possible, and she eventually gave in, and they admitted her to the hospital. I stopped in a flower shop before going down to visit her and I had a vision of her laying with her eyes closed in a white room. I called her on the way there and asked what they had found out, and she reluctantly told me that she had cancer and would need to have surgery.

In a few short months after that, my dad died suddenly alongside the road. Though the dream was an unsettling and horrific encounter, it was part of a greater plan and purpose, and it was meant to warn and prepare me as much as possible for what was to come. I remain grateful for that experience to this day.

Guy said that prior to having this dream, there were other dream experiences pointing to the passing of both his father. However, the dreams mixed identities because he shared the same name as his father and grandfather. The dreams also contained astrological symbolism:

I had a dream where my parents and I were standing up from my grandparents' house and I noticed a wand laying on the ground. When I picked up the wand it snapped in my hand and revealed the 12 signs of the zodiac, and I looked up to see the eye of God towering over us in the sky, weeping tears of fire.

I had told my dad a year prior to this particular dream that he would have a strong possibility of death when Uranus entered Aries, where both our Moons are placed natally and also my Rising sign, and Saturn was conjunct my natal Sun. So I took the dream to mean at that time that they [parents] would both suffer acts of God that I would be powerless to stop. I also experienced high anxiety and became very ill physically in the summer months prior to all that happened in the fall of 2011.

I had another dream where a friend was looking at my natal birth chart and told me that I was going to die that year (2011). After my dad passed, she shared with me that she had a dream that I was laying in a white casket. It recurred up to the time that he passed away.

My mom also had a dream of my father that he was in the family cemetery sitting on top of a white casket as we were planning his funeral, just my friend had seen in her dream.

We deduced that my friend had dreamed of me in the casket and I had dreamed of her predicting my death because I was named after my dad and grandfather.

Impending death of unknown persons

Dreams may give warnings of an imminent death but not reveal the identity of the person who will die. My mother, who had numerous precognitive dreams often involving deaths, sometimes was not given the full picture. For example, she had such a dream about two weeks before President John F. Kennedy was assassinated in Dallas, on November 22, 1963. In the dream, she was standing on a street in a large crowd of people, watching a solemn procession. She knew it was a funeral cortege, and someone important had died. She saw her own dead mother in the crowd, and felt nauseated in the dream. Upon awakening, the nausea was still with her.

For Mother, there were two unmistakable signs that this dream foretold a death: the presence of her own dead mother, and the physical discomfort. These were her personal "markers" that were present in precognitive death warning dreams that distinguished these dreams from ordinary ones.

However, Mother did not know who was going to die, or when. Two weeks later, she watched President Kennedy's funeral procession on the streets of Washington, D.C., and recognized the scenes from her dream.

In a more personal case, Mother had another forewarning dream with the same "markers," in which she received the message that "Don has died of a heart attack." My father's name was Don, and he did have a heart condition. At the time, he was working in another state on a job, and Mother worried that he was going to have a fatal heart attack. About two weeks later—the window of warning time that my mother usually had with these dreams—she received word that the husband of a close friend in another state, whose name was also Don, died of a heart attack.

As noted, my mother's deceased mother often served as the messenger of an impending death. The appearances of the dead in dreams do not automatically carry that meaning, but in some cases they do foreshadow a passing. It all depends on context.

Like Guy's case, Mother's dream was right with the name, but did not specify the right person with the name. Displacement of details and timing is common in precognition. One notable example of this is a dream about the Apollo 12 moon mission in 1969 had by the gifted psychic Alan Vaughan. The dream did not involve the dead, but its details illustrate how precognitive dreams can be "nearly right."

Vaughan was one of the principal subjects among the 100 people tested for telepathic dreaming in the famous research conducted at the Maimonides Medical Center in Brooklyn, New York. He co-authored the book about the research, *Dream Telepathy: Experiments in Nocturnal ESP*, with researchers Montague Ullman and Stanley Krippner, two individuals well-known for their work in dreams and in altered states of consciousness.

Prior to the Apollo 12 mission, Vaughan meditated on it. He had a dream in which he saw grave danger for the mission—if something in electrical or fuel system was not fixed, there would be an explosion that could kill the astronauts. He saw an image of astronaut Neil Armstrong's footprint on the moon, with a big X crossing it out. With that came the certain feeling that the mission would not reach the moon.

On takeoff, the rocket carrying Apollo 12 was struck by lightning, causing a problem. It was fixed, and the mission reached the moon and returned without further mishap. It seemed that Vaughan had accurately tuned in the an electrical problem—the lightning—but had been wrong about the overall fate of the mission.

Four months later, Apollo 13 launched for another moon mission. As the ship left the Earth's orbit, there was a big explosion of fuel. Most of the ship's electricity was cut off. The lives and safe return of the astronauts were in jeopardy. Tension was high as NASA ground control and the astronauts tried to figure out a solution. The moon landing was aborted. A plan was conceived to use the moon's gravitational field as a slingshot to help propel the crippled ship back to Earth. The plan worked, and the astronauts were able to return home in safety.

Vaughan had been both wrong and right. He saw the circumstances of Apollo 13, but associated them with Apollo 12 because of his meditation on that particular mission.

Death eyes

Ariel was five years old when her sister, age six, died. The family worked through their sorrow and trauma. Ariel had no dreams featuring her sister until 20 years later, when she appeared as a messenger of death:

> I was at Niagara Falls. My best friend was with me and we were walking along the walkway towards the falls. The mist from the falls was hitting our faces. We were having a good time laughing and in good spirits.
>
> All of a sudden I had this urge to turn around and when I did, I saw my sister. I looked straight at her and she had these dark piercing eyes. She was the age she was when she died, and had her communion dress on. Nothing was said. But at that moment I saw her I woke up. I was terrified. I got out of bed and went through the house and turned all the lights on, and was in a state of shock.

My first thought was, "My God, that can't be, she died." Not once in 20 years did I ever see her, and here she appears out of the blue. Her eyes were as I call them death eyes, very dark and ominous. I believed that something was going to happen but I did not know to whom or when or what—it was just very frightening, almost like she was actually in my room.

Shortly after this dream, my brother-in-law was killed in a car accident.

Ariel has received no more warning dreams involving her sister, even though other members of the family have passed away. She wondered why her sister seemed to warn of the death of someone she had never met. Others ask similar questions about odd or incomplete warning dreams. Sometimes there are no adequate answers. Certain conditions may need to be in place for interdimensional dreams to transmit and be received, and some of the conditions are unique to the souls involved. We do not yet understand all of the mechanisms involved in dreaming that are beyond the physiological ones that can be studied scientifically. There are emotional, spiritual and subtle energy factors involved.

Interpreting warning dreams

Dreams of dying and death can be symbolic rather than literal, and one must be careful in interpreting them. Once precognitive dreams happen is fate sealed? There are no clear answers. There are documented cases of precognitive dreams saving lives, such as people who avoid travel and thereby avoid fatal accidents. For example, despite massive publicity, the superliner Titanic sailed without a full passenger load on its maiden voyage from England to New York in April 1912. Some passengers who were booked cancelled because they had dreams that the ship was doomed; others had "bad feelings" about going; and for others, events intervened that prevented them from going. Yet no one reported dreaming that the ship would strike an iceberg and sink, killing 1502 of the 2207 passengers on board.

Perhaps the purpose of forewarning dreams is more to prepare rather than prevent, as part of the unfoldment of life, death and the afterlife.

10

Dreams of the Dying

Dreams help people to anticipate and prepare for their transition to the afterlife. Individuals who have terminal illness or who die in old age often experience changes in their dreams as they get closer to death. Moving toward a certain end to one's life can be a difficult psychological and emotional process, and dreams provide a powerful calming and healing force. They open a window into the afterlife, providing previews of the new world at hand. Marie-Louise von Franz, a psychotherapist and a pupil of Jung, noted in her book *On Dreams and Death*:

> The dreams of dying people are not about death, but usually about a journey. They have to get ready for a journey, or they have to go through a dark tunnel and be reborn into another world, or they have to go through a disagreeable darkness or through a dark cloud to come out into another space, or they are finally going to meet their beloved partner.

Dreams of a long journey, especially by boat across vast expanses of water, are a common transition dream. They evoke ancient associations of realms separated by water, such as the rivers that encircled Hades in Greek mythology. To get to the land of the dead, souls had to cross the River Styx.

Terminally ill patients often have transitional dreams close to the time of dying, usually within two weeks. Transition symbols include going through gateways, entering beautiful gardens, crossing bridges, climbing mountains, traversing the sea in a boat or ferry, setting off down a long river, or walking through doorways. They dream of reunions with the dead, including their pets, and also of being greeted and guided by spiritual helpers, such as angels. Sometimes the dying dream of seeing thmeslves gradually restored to health and vitality.

Preparation dreams often are vivid in colors, and permeated with emotions of love and tranquility. They are real to the dreamer, and bring profound peace of mind.

These dream symbols are not limited to death transition dreams, of course, and can appear in ordinary dreaming about daily life. Symbols and themes must be interpreted within context.

Dreams of the dying relate to closures in all aspects of life as well. In *Final Gifts: Understanding the Special Awareness, Needs, and Communications of the Dying*, hospice nurses Maggie Callanan and Patricia Kelley describe the process as "Nearing Death Awareness," which includes accepting death, coming to terms with their lives, dealing with anxieties and fears, and resolving unfinished personal issues and business. Dreams play an important role in the process, revealing valuable information that can benefit all persons concerned, including surviving family members and friends.

Fears about dying surface in dreams. For example, in *Final Gifts* a woman named Isabelle had a repeating dream of being buried alive in a coffin. She knew exactly what it meant: she had a real fear of being pronounced dead while she was still alive. This fear is not uncommon. Discussing the dream enabled others to explain to Isabelle precisely how death is determined, and that there would be no doubt when the end came. After that she was greatly relieved and the repeating dream ceased.

Stages of dying

Like dreams of grief and mourning, dreams of the dying move through stages as well. One case in my files concerns a woman's mother who was dying of cancer. Initially she dreamed repeatedly of finding her beloved garden in stages of death and decay; nothing could be made to grow there. Toward the end of her illness, she dreamed of finding new shoots of growth in her garden.

Initial dreams of the dying may emphasize images of death and decay, especially of vegetation and animals; things coming to an end and the stopping or freezing of time-keeping pieces like watches and clocks. These images have potent healing power to help the patient come to terms with what is happening to them. The dreams themselves usher in a new stage of consciousness.

The element of light

A dominant image in dreams of the dying is light: darkness is illuminated with light or turns into light; a new light shines. (Light also is dominant in dreams of the dead—the deceased often appear swathed in radiance or seemingly emanating light from within.)

In *Dreams: God's Forgotten Language*, John Sanford gives this dream of a dying Protestant clergyman:

> ...he sees the clock on the mantelpiece; the hands have been moving, but now they stop; as they stop, a window opens behind the mantelpiece clock and a bright light shines through. The opening widens into a door and the light becomes a brilliant path. He walks out onto the path of light and disappears.

Doors and windows are symbols of portals into new worlds. A path, like a river, takes us on a journey through a landscape.

In *On Dreams and Death*, Marie-Louise von Franz tells this dream of a young woman with brain cancer. The dream occurred the day before she died:

> I am standing beside my bed in the hospital room and I feel strong and healthy. Sunshine flows in through the window. The doctor is there and says, "Well, Miss X, you are unexpectedly completely cured. You may get dressed and leave the hospital." At that moment I turn around and see, lying in the bed—my own dead body!

The dream presaged the imminent transition from life into death and the afterlife. In the dream this is heralded by the sunshine that floods through the window. Von Franz rejected the idea of this dream as a wish fulfillment for a cure. The dream speaks to a holistic healing on a soul level, a readiness to embrace a new life.

Invisible helpers

Also common are experiences in which the dying person spends more and more time in the company of others who are dead, or who seem to be spiritual beings, such as angels, who have come to help them make their transition. Such experiences occur in dreams, borderland states of consciousness and waking visions, all of which are very real to the experiencer. Dreams and visionary experiences of the dying should not be treated as hallucinations, but given proper attention. Sometimes as death nears, the patient spends more and more time aware of an invisible world and invisible presences.

Heavenly music

Angelic choirs and beautiful singing are heard by the dying. An account from 19th-century Ireland was made by a man who was visiting a woman dying of a long illness. She heard singing and also saw a dead friend:

I was sitting at the foot of her bed talking over some business matters that she was anxious to arrange, being perfectly composed and in thorough possession of her senses; in fact, she was right, and my solicitor, who advised that the step she wanted to be taken was not necessary, was wrong. She changed the subject and said, "Do you hear those voices singing?" I replied that I did not; and she said, "I have heard them several times today, and I am sure they are angels welcoming me to Heaven; but," she added, "it is strange, there is one voice amongst them I am sure I know and cannot remember whose voice it is." Suddenly she stopped and said, pointing straight over my head, "Why, there she is in the corner of the room; it is Julia X., she is coming on; she is leaning over you; she has her hands up; she is praying; do look; she is going." I turned but could not see anything. Mrs. _____ then said, "She is gone."

The woman died the following day. Her father reported that she "began singing in the morning, and sang and sang until she died."

Deathbed visions

Related to dreams of the dying are deathbed visions, experiences that happen close to death. The dying describe what they see around them: the dead, religious and spiritual figures, brilliant colors, bright light, and beautiful scenes.

Deathbed visions have been recorded since ancient times, but were not scientifically studied until the late 19th century. According to more recent studies, about 10 percent of people are conscious prior to their death, and about 50-67 percent of them have one or more deathbed visions. The visions have common characteristics that cut across racial, cultural, religious, educational, age and socio-economic lines.

Early research

Early psychical researchers, including Frederic W.H. Myers, Edmund Gurney, Frank Podmore and James H. Hyslop, documented cases of deathbed visions in the late 19th and early20th centuries. The first comprehensive study was done in the early 20th century by Sir William Barrett, a distinguished professor of physics at the Royal College of Science in Dublin and a psychical researcher.

Barrett's interest in deathbed visions was piqued in 1924 when his wife, a physician specializing in obstetrical surgery, told him about a woman patient who spoke of seeing visions of a place of great beauty and her dead father and sister shortly before she died. The visions were real to the patient, and transformed her into a state of great radiance and peace. When shown her baby, she pondered staying for its sake, then said, "I can't stay; if you could see what I do, you would know I can't stay." What struck Barrett was the fact that the woman had not known her sister had died about three weeks earlier, yet she saw her sister with her dead father.

Several decades later, Barrett's research interested Karlis Osis, then director of research for Eileen J. Garrett's Parapsychology Foundation. Osis also had his own personal experience motivating him to undertake the research. In 1932, at age 15, he was struck by tuberculosis. At that time, tuberculosis was a serious and potentially fatal disease, whose main cure consisted of bed-rest, fresh air and good nutrition. At dusk one evening, his room was suddenly filled with light and a wave of joy swept over him. A moment later the door opened and a relative announced, "Auntie just died." Osis had just experienced a farewell visit from the newly dead. He saw no vision of his aunt, but experienced the intense wave of energy of her transition.

Under the auspices of the Parapsychology Foundation in 1959-60, and later the American Society for Psychical Research (ASPR) from 1961-1964 and 1972-73, Osis collected information from doctors and nurses on tens of thousands of deathbed and near-death experiences in the United States and India. The Indian survey (1972-73) was conducted with Erlendur Haraldsson. Of those cases, more than 1,000 were examined in detail. The findings of these studies confirmed Barrett's findings, as well as the experiences of individuals who work with the terminally ill and dying. The findings also are in agreement with many of the findings of NDE research.

Characteristics of deathbed visions

Deathbed visions most frequently occur to individuals who die gradually, such as from terminal illness or serious injuries, rather than those who die suddenly, such as from heart attacks.

The majority of visions are of apparitions of the dead, who often are glowing and dressed in white. They usually are close family members, such as parents, children, siblings or spouses. They may be accompanied by beings of light perceived as mythical, spiritual or religious figures or deities, for example: angels, Jesus, the Virgin Mary, Krishna, Yama (the Hindu god of death) Yamhoot (the messenger of Yama), or similar figures. Sometimes the religious and spiritual figures come alone.

Psychical researchers call these figures "take-away apparitions," because they beckon or command the dying to come with them, as if they have come to assist in the transition to the afterlife. The response of most of the dying is one of happiness and willingness to go, especially if the individual believes in an afterlife (deathbed visions also occur to those who do not believe in an afterlife). If the patient has been in great pain or depression, a complete turnaround of mood is observed, and pain vanishes. The dying one literally seems to "light up" with radiance. If family and friends are in attendance, they may mistake this sudden energy as a sign of a miraculous recovery.

The appearance of take-away apparitions is an infallible sign of impending or imminent death. They appear to patients who are expected to recover, but once visited by the take-away figure, succumb. Sometimes take-away figures make their first appearances a week or two before death, and appear with increasing frequency as the time of transition nears.

The living usually do not see these figures. "Grandpa is here!" a patient may exclaim. "He's right there—can't you see him?" They will nod and smile as though responding to communications, and, if they are able, may even answer back, in what the living hear as a one-way conversation. They may make statements such as, "Mom is here," I've got to go now," and then fall into sleep. As patients become less responsive, they may fix their attention in a certain part of their room, as though they are seeing something. Frequently they will look up and make comments about the world they see "up there."

Most deathbed vision are short in duration. According to Osis and Haraldsson, about half of them last five minutes or less. Another 17 percent last 6-15 minutes; and 17 percent last more than one hour. Approximately 76 percent of the patients studied died within 10 minutes of their afterlife vision, and nearly all of the rest died within one or several hours. In a few cases, one or more visions were seen by a patient over the course of several days, as though they were announcing appointments with death at a certain time. The appearance of the vision seems to have little connection with the physical condition of the patient. Some who seemed to be recovering and then had visions and then quickly fell into comas and died.

Visions of the afterlife

Minutes before dying, scenes of the afterlife may unfold. Approximately one-third of deathbed visions involve total visions, in which the patient sees the Other Side, which appears real and tangible to them, as though the physical reality melts away and is replaced by another world. Sometimes the patient feels transported out of body to the location.

The most common descriptions are of endless gardens of great beauty. Some also see gates, bridges, rivers, boats and other symbols of transition, as well as castles and other architectural structures. Regardless of what they show, the visions are resplendent with intense, vivid colors and bright light. There may be other beings present in the landscape, including dead people known to the experiencer, and spiritual beings such as angels. The emotional response of the patient is usually one of happiness and anticipation at going to the beautiful place. Some examples cited by Osis and Haraldsson:

> She said the gates of heaven were opening. There were shining tall portals and there was shining light, much brighter than here. Everything looked so bright.

> ...beautiful surroundings where green grass and flowers grow. She seemed very pleased, happy that she could see these pleasant things. She said it was like a garden with green grass and flowers. She was fond of flowers and had a garden at home.

> Suddenly his face lit up, pain gone, smiling—he hadn't been cheerful until then. He said, "How beautiful," as if he could see something we couldn't see. And then, "No body, no world, flowers, light and my Mary [deceased wife]." He was released and peaceful, went into a coma and died shortly after.

> ...he saw Christ coming down through the air very slowly. Christ called him, rather waved his hand that he should come to him. Then Christ disappeared and he [the patient] was fully here. The patient told me he would die within a few minutes. He seemed quite happy and said the aim of his life had been achieved by Christ calling him to Him. "I am going," he said, and departed a few minutes later.

> He saw his deceased mother and sister, was surprised but pleased to see them. I was surprised to learn that his sister and mother were dead. He was so natural with them that I thought they were alive at home. "Hello, it's good to see you..." he would say. Afterwards, he was perfectly clear with full memory of his relatives' visit.

A small number of those studied in the Osis-Haraldsson research heard heavenly music as well:

> He heard the angels singing and music. He felt like he was floating.

Deathbed visions and religion

Studies have found that few of these visions (17 percent in the Osis-Haraldsson study) conform to religious teachings about the nature of the afterlife. Osis and Haraldsson found only one case of a vision described as hell, from a Catholic woman who seemed to be carrying a great burden of guilt about her perceived sins.

"Belief in life after death and involvement in religion do not change the content of the visions but significantly increase the symbolization of death and reaction with religious emotions," Osis and Haraldsson said.

Similarity to NDEs and dreams

Deathbed visions are similar to near-death experiences in which the experiencer enters a reality of sacred space and is flooded with feelings of great peace and elation, and sees similar figures and scenes.

They are similar to afterlife dreams in which imagery is vivid, lucid and otherworldly, and features the dead and spiritual beings. Communication takes place that is meant for the experiencer.

Sensations of being out-of-body occur in all three experiences.

Explanations for deathbed visions

Researchers have examined natural explanations to account for deathbed visions, such as the effects of drugs (many dying persons are on narcotic pain killers), fever, hallucinations caused by oxygen deprivation in the brain, depersonalization that occurs during dying, and even wish fulfillment for a continuation of life somewhere. These explanations have also been advanced for NDEs, and some of them for dreams (medications, wish fulfillments).

None satisfactorily explain deathbed visions. When these other conditions can cause hallucinations, they are found not to concern the afterlife, but to relate mostly to the present. The Osis-Haraldsson research found that deathbed visions are most likely to occur in patients who are fully conscious and not heavily medicated. Thus, medical factors are not likely to cause true deathbed visions. They also ruled out wish-fulfillment as a likely explanation, as the visions do not conform to expectations of patients, religious or otherwise, and appear even to those who want to recover and live.

Visions of the soul's departure

Related to a deathbed vision seen by the dying is another type of deathbed vision that is witnessed by the living who are in attendance to the dying. As the person dies, clouds of white or silvery energy rise and float over the body. In some cases, the energy forms into the astral body of the dying one, connected by a silvery cord which drops or dissipates at the moment of death.

Sometimes the form is seen to be escorted away by other forms that are recognized as the dead, angels or spiritual beings. From a hospice nurse:

> When it became clear that the time was near for [the patient], the family gathered around the bed to see him through to the end. A strange calm and peace settled over the room. The moment he was gone, I saw a whitish, cloud of mist form over his body. The cloud hovered over him for a few seconds and then rose into the air and out of sight. One of the family members saw it, too.

Visual experiences of the soul's departure were more common in earlier times when more people died at home. They are not as often reported in hospital settings, but they are in hospice settings. Perhaps familiar surroundings better enable witnesses to have the experience.

The wholeness of life and death

While dreams of the dying do point to certain themes, there are no "definitive" dreams that announce death. Among the commonly shared images and symbols are images and symbols that are as varied as individual dreamers, and relate to personal context just as do "ordinary" dreams. Sometimes dreams of death may relate to our need to confront the subject or fear of death. Death dreams also may address symbolic deaths, such as the ending of something important in the life of the dreamer.

Jung observed that the worlds of the living and dead form a whole. Our physical and psychic energy is the same; during life it is contained in physical form, and then it makes a transformation in death to the psychic, which is unbounded by time and space.

Our dreams and visions of dying, death and the dead are as important to our wholeness as are the dreams about our stresses, anxieties, emotions, healing, creativity, spiritual initiations, turning points and experiences of God. Dying is a part of living. Jung observed that our birth is a death and our death is a birth. Our dreams deal with the full spectrum of our existence, of our coming and going in different forms.

Dreams of the dead, death and dying can raise powerful emotions, and they should not be ignored. Sometimes a professional therapist or counselor should be consulted. People who care for the dying should be especially alert for dreams that are vivid, recurring or in a series that seems to be progressive. Dreams should be discussed, and the dreamer should be invited to freely interpret the dream. Often this can provide an opportunity for a dying person to discuss anxieties that he she might otherwise be reluctant to broach.

Health care workers, physicians, clergy, counselors and others who assist the dying should be educated about dreamwork and dreams of the dying, as well as deathbed visions, near-death experiences, out-of-body experiences, and other forms of after-death communications, in order to help people process the emotional and spiritual content of their experiences.

In particular, dreams can be powerful forces to relieve fears of dying and to validate personal beliefs about the continuation of life in another realm.

11

A Dream Journey Through Life and Death

For years before he died, author Michael Talbot had dreams of meetings with Death and previewing the afterlife. From an early age, he was deeply in tune with himself and spiritual forces through his dreams. His dreams prepared him for many of his extraordinary life experiences, and paved the way for his exit from life into the afterlife. Talbot believed in reincarnation, and some of his impending death dreams related to rebirth.

Talbot had a fine talent as a bestselling author of both nonfiction and fiction works. His career and life were cut short in 1992, when he died at age 38 of chronic lymphoscystic leukemia. Among his works are *Mysticism and the New Physics*, *Beyond the Quantum*, *The Reincarnation Handbook*, several novels, and *The Holographic Universe*, his last book.

In 1988, while I was researching my book *Tales of Reincarnation*, I had several conversations with Michael, and once spent an afternoon with him at his New York City apartment conducting a taped interview. There was a mysterious quality about Michael, as though he perceived realms that few people ever glimpsed. He was a psychic lightning rod himself, having had some experiences early in life that seemed to have opened his psychic channels. Our conversation covered a range of topics beyond reincarnation, including some unusual dreams that he had experienced beginning at an early age.

"My dreams are very important to me," said Michael, "and I am constantly watching them for their clues and guidance. Some dreams are just dreams, but others have a valance that you know they are something more."

One early experience in particular seemed to set the stage for the course his life would follow:

> As a child I had a very moving experience. I don't know if it was a dream or a vision. It was in memory as an actual experience, but I could not remember where it began or where it ended. When I was about three or four, an entity came to me. I thought it was a woman, but in retrospect it could have been androgynous. It was a stereotypical guide figure with a long robe and white hair. It was taking me by the hand through the woods at night. At the time, we lived in Michigan, and the landscape seemed to be near where we lived.
>
> I thought, "This has got to be my mother," although I knew deep in my heart it wasn't, but I would have been too panicked to think otherwise.
>
> The entity took me to the shore of a lake and said, "Are you afraid, Michael?"
>
> I said, "Yes."
>
> She said, "Hold your hand upward palm toward the moon." I did that. She said, "Now close your hand."
>
> As I did I could feel the air, like when you hold your hand out of a car window, but there was no wind, there was just a softness.
>
> The being said, "Do you feel that?"
>
> I said, "Yes."
>
> She said, "There is something I want you always to remember. No matter what happens to you in your life, don't ever be afraid. For you the darkness is soft."
>
> It was always a very comforting message to me. Later I thanked my mother for the experience. She said, "You're welcome," but she had no

memory of taking me through the woods—she just passed me off as a child.

When Michael was five, he had a shared UFO encounter with his parents and friends during a camping trip. On their way to get food, his father and a male adult friend saw a green ball of light land in the woods. He said:

> They stopped, thinking it was going to set the woods on fire. Out of the woods came this entity—a human in a long, white robe with long white hair. They came back to the campsite and got me, my mother, and my dad's friend's wife, and took us back there. We all watched this entity for quite some time. I had a clear sense that this was the [same] "woman in white" as I called her. My dad wanted to go up and talk to her, but my mother and panicked and said no. We finally drove away. My dad later went back with another neighbor and found footprints which could have conceivably been human but were anomalous. They were very tiny and very, very narrow, like baby feet, little slats almost. He took photographs which unfortunately have since gotten lost.

A psychic friend of Michael's told him the "woman in white" was a guide from another level of reality who had come to give a sort of blessing. "Something happened to you that had to do with your bones at around age 14," he told Michael. "Had she not blessed you, you would have died, but as it was, it developed into the problem that it did." Michael had never shared with the psychic that he had scoliosis—a curvature of the spine—and that he spent about five years in a spine brace.

Michael had other exceptional experiences throughout life, including a poltergeist-like spirit who tagged along with him wherever he lived.

I was particularly interested in his dreams that involved death and the Other Side, including this out-of-body dream encounters with Death:

I had several vivid dreams encountering Death, including one where I was taken to the pre-death state, I believe. I knew [in waking life] that I was having a struggle with my life. The dream started out with a woman saying to me, "Will you pray with me?" She had a live ferret on one arm and a white owl on the other. She said, "While we are praying, I want you to watch these animals, and if one of them turns into a human being you must talk to it."

I said, "Yes, I understand."

So we were praying and I was keeping an eye on these animals, and the owl reached out to me. At first I was frightened because I thought it was going to nip my ears, and I pulled back. Then I thought it was asking me "lend me your ear," so I let it take a hold of my ear and it turned into a woman. She was short, a bit stocky. Her presence was very wise, loving, powerful and positive.

She said, "I'm going to take you somewhere."

I said, "Okay."

We went through this instant transition where suddenly we were in a very large room full of people. They all seemed rather excited. She introduced me to them and said, "This is Michael and he's in college."

I thought that was amusing because I had been out of college for some time. I said, "No, I'm not in college."

She said, "Yes, you are, you don't understand. You're in college on terra firma." She pulled on my sport jacket and said, "Judging from the way you are dressed, I would say somewhere on the East Coast." Then I realized that she was talking about being in the earth life.

Two young boys came up to me—they must have been about 14 or 15—and they said, "We're about to go—what is it like?"

I couldn't really answer. I said, "It's what you make of it. It's wonderful or awful depending on what you make of it."

They said, "We're really looking forward to it," and I realized they were waiting to be born. I think most of the people in the room were about to be born.

The woman said, "Now you've got to shake hands with someone." I turned around and there was a strange-looking man coming toward me. He was bald and heavy set, very pale. The first thing I noticed was that his wrists had double joints in them. They were like tree limbs, very creepy looking.

She said, "You've got to shake his hand."

I said, "I don't want to shake his hand."

She said, "That's all right, he doesn't want to shake yours." So I shook his hand, and it was ice cold and clammy. I said, "Oh, it's like something out of a crypt!"

She said, "You've got that exactly right."

At that point, I realized he was Death.

He said, "Do you want to go with me?"

I said, "No, I don't."

He said, "Then you must consider something."

"What's that?" I said.

He said, "What are your resources?"

After I heard that I knew that I had the wherewithal within me to decide whether I was living or dying. The Death figure looked almost passive and weak, like he could not overpower me and make me go with him.

The woman then said to me—she seemed to be sort of a psychic guide, she had a very powerful, glistening presence— she said, "I'm going to send you back now, but there's something I want you to remember. From time to time I'm going to send you beautiful books. You'll know they will have come from me because they will be so beautiful."

I did not know what that prediction meant, but it was kind of magical.

The next thing I knew, I was sailing through levels of reality. It was like swiftly passing by rock strata—each one was there for just a moment. But I could see an incredible distance, far vaster than it seemed an earth horizon should be. At first I thought I was looking at integrated circuitry, because there was something so geometric and beautiful and colorful about the vista. Then I realized that I was looking at cities, but not earth cities. They were celestial, beautiful, alien, exotic cities, in very deep, rich colors, indigoes, blues, reds, purples. There were a lot of purples, although each one was different. The lights were glistening yellow like street lights. I could see a vast geometry of streets, but it was more complex than normal city streets. There were mountain ranges, sweeping, almost lunar-looking, not stark but alien and very rich. I didn't see any foliage or plants, but everything had a sense of richness.

I was mesmerized by what was happening to me. They came one right after another, bam bam bam bam, zooming past, and then bam, I hit my body with a jerk.

This dream was rich in potent symbols, all presaging Michael's transition out of earthly life. The woman was a guide figure, and her instruction to pray may have pointed to a need for Michael to address his interior life, to get his inner affairs in order. The ferret represented discovery through investigation ("ferreting out" information) and the owl represented wisdom. The owl became a woman (feminine wisdom, or the voice of the anima) in order to speak. Owls also have a strange connection to entity contact experiences, and often show up in extraterrestrial encounters.

The place that Michael called "pre-death" resembled descriptions of the "between-life" or "intermission" state in the literature pertaining to reincarnation memories: rooms or buildings filled with souls awaiting their next incarnation on earth, or newly deceased souls awaiting integration into the afterlife.

Michael interpreted the books in the dream as new systems of knowledge that he would encounter. Indeed, until the end of his life, he absorbed himself in a study of the subjects he loved so much: mysticism, consciousness, science, and the Eternal.

The rushing through levels of reality and seeing cities of light occurs in lucid and out-of-body dreams and also in near-death experiences. Otherworldly cities of light are described in the literature of mystics and shamans as well. The mystic Emmanuel Swedenborg (discussed in the next chapter) described visiting brilliant cities of staggering architecture and beauty during his dream-like experiences.

In many descriptions, the cities are vast in size. They glow with a light that seems to emanate from within. They seem to be made literally from gold and silver that have an unearthly translucence or sheen. The cities are filled with enormous buildings, such as libraries that dreamers know house all of the records of the universe (the Akashic Records). The following description comes from the files of NDE researcher Kenneth Ring, a description provided by an experiencer:

> ...suddenly there was this tremendous burst of light and... I was turned... to the light. I saw in the distance a great city... And then I began to realize that the light was coming from within this city and there just seemed to be a laser beam of light and in the midst of that, that was directed to me. And I just rode that laser beam of light through a vastness, being aware that there were other life forms going by... Oh, tremendous speed, tremendous speed... I just went right down into [the city]... Everything was very defined, on the one hand, but it also had a blending with everything else. The flowers and the flower buds by that street—the intensity, the vibrant colors, like pebbles that have been polished in a running stream, but they were all like precious stones, rubies and diamonds and sapphires...

Michael's dream also foreshadowed an impending health crisis, which occurred around Easter time in 1988. "I had my own little resurrection," Michael said. "I got very ill and was in the hospital for 10 days. They didn't think I was going to survive, but I pulled through." Michael remained ill for several weeks. During that time he had more dream encounters with Death:

> I had three dreams in which Death came to me. The first dream was very simple. I was on a desolate, desert-like landscape at night, and a train came by. I knew immediately that it was a death train. The conductor looked spectral. He said, "This is the night train—would you like to get

on?"

I said, "No."

I had a very clear understanding that were I to get on, I would have died—it was taking souls away.

The last dream took place a few days before my recovery. The scene looked like Mexico City at night, with a lot of wrought iron gates. I knew I was being pursued by a psychopath. I'd had a glimpse of him. He was a young man, his hair was very disheveled, and he was glistening with sweat. He had glassy eyes and he was totally mad. I knew he meant my death, and that if I were to confront him, I would be dead instantly. I was trying to get away. I had a beautiful estate that I had to leave and go through these wrought iron gates into the city, which was labrythine and like a surrealist painting. The whole thing was Kafka-esque, with this psychopath after me.

I managed to get back to my estate. I was coming down this street and I knew I had to shut the gate. I shut it, but it was making too much sound. I didn't want to attract his attention, so I left it without locking it, and I hid in a Rolls Royce that was in the courtyard. I heard him come in. I was crouched down below the window. I heard his feet crunching in the gravel all around the car. Then he went out. I heard the gate close. I got up.

Another man was there. I didn't sense any menace from him. He gave me a bone with Anubis's head carved on it. He said, "This one is for you—it's from that man who was just here."

I realized that the psychopath had represented Death, which was Anubis, and I had been through the gates of the underworld, and that he had almost got me. When I had come back in to the estate, the game was over, and he was saying, "Here, you have your life back, I have gone back to my world."

That was the third encounter with Death, and shortly after that I recovered.

The setting of Mexico City has associations with the realm of the dead, with its famous annual festival, the Day of the Dead in May, in which the ancestral spirits are honored. In Egyptian mythology, Anubis is the jackal-headed god who leads the souls of the newly dead into the Underworld. Gates, as Michael observed, represent portals of transition, in this case, from earthly life to the after-death state. The estate represented Michael's earthly life.

The series of three dreams (Michael did not share the details of the second dream; he thought the first and third were the most significant) pointed to another gateway, one through which Michael eventually would pass for the final time. Several years later, his illness got the upper hand, and Michael could no longer outrun and outsmart Death.

I have often wondered about his last dreams, and the mysteries of the Eternal they must have shown him.

12

Previews of the Afterlife

All of us wonder what will happen to us when we die. We take comfort from our religious and spiritual beliefs, and perhaps from the experiences of others who say they have seen the Other Side. For many of us, however, the Great Mystery remains the Great Fear.

Our questions about life after death are sometimes answered in dreams. We are shown places, usually of great beauty, and given stories about activities there. The Talmud holds that during sleep, one's soul rises into heavens and amuses itself with God.

A powerful dream about the Other Side can have a tremendous effect on releasing fear of death and satisfying our need for reassurance concerning the world that awaits us when our final breath is drawn. Such dreams can occur any time in life, but are especially likely to happen during times of stress or inner struggle, or prior to our actual death. It should be noted that a dream of the hereafter does not necessarily presage one's death. Ordinary dreams can use the symbolism of the afterlife in order to address deep spiritual or philosophical matters.

Carl G. Jung related the story of one of his pupils, a 60-year-old woman who had a dream of the afterlife about two months prior to her death:

> She had entered the hereafter. There was a class going on, and various deceased women friends of hers sat at the front bench. An atmosphere of general expectation prevailed. She looked around for a teacher or lecturer, but could find none. Then it became plain that she herself was the lecturer, for immediately after death people had to give accounts of the total experience of their lives. The dead were extremely interested in the life experiences that the newly deceased brought with them, just as if the acts and experiences taking place in earthly life, in space and time, were the decisive ones.

At the time of the dream, the woman was fearful of death. Jung did not comment on the effect of the dream upon her, but noted that the dream provided a myth about death and the richness of the land of the dead, which can be reassuring.

The process of dying

Professional psychic John Russell once shared a dream with me in which the process of dying was described. Russell is accustomed to receiving communications from the dead in readings he gives to clients. On one occasion, a woman came through in an "amazing dream" he had to share her experience of dying:

> In this dream, I was giving a psychic reading to a man who had recently lost his mother, and was agonizingly bereaved. His mother was coming through to me from the other side, which is a normal occurrence when I give psychic readings. I've also seen ghosts, sometimes physically solid, and she appeared to me in my dream during this reading, but her son couldn't see her. She then told me to tell him something for her, and

what she related to me I've never heard expressed quite this way! She was talking about how it was for her to die, and she said, "You know how when you're driving your car, and you look down and the gas gauge is on empty, and you know you're going to run out of gas? At that moment, you have this feeling, this certainty, that you're going to run out of gas, and there's nothing you can do about it. And, you know when the car stalls and you coast it to a stop, the only option you then have is to get out of the car and walk for help, to the nearest gas station. That's how it was when I died. I knew, with clarity and certainty, that at that moment, my "vehicle," my body, had "run out of gas." And I also realized that my only option was to exit that vehicle, and walk for help, go for help, that is...to make my transition. And at that moment, let me tell you that I was absolutely conscious, totally coherent, totally aware. I've never been more lucid. And at the moment of transition, I have never experienced such a feeling of total and complete peace and well being."

The dream was realistic, like a waking consciousness experience. It left John "pleasantly astonished." The woman's explanation of her transition made perfect sense.

Going to the Park

Many dreams and visions about the afterlife reveal a pleasant, park-like or garden setting permeated by an atmosphere of peace and tranquility. Tom W. was granted such a glimpse of the Other Side after meditating upon the question of life after death for a prolonged period of time during an inner crisis about his spiritual and religious beliefs. He explained:

In the year prior to this dream, my world views had radically changed. I had been a theology major for a year when I had a profound change of heart and left my faith. The change of heart concerned the issue of whether or not anyone—a person or a religion—could be the judge of the spiritual state of another human being. I was being taught how my religion was right and others were misguided. Suddenly I could not see how an infinite

God could require all people of the world to see one particular message as being the only right one, and threaten to kill them later in a second resurrection if they did not accept this truth. Rather, most people were involved in a deep inner psychology of their own, which seemed rather real to me. What I was doing seemed unreal compared to the lives of others that I had either interacted with or read about.

However, instead of believing that a more rational, personal element to the universe existed, I immediately assumed that there was no God and that humanity existed as the result of a bunch of chemical reactions that would eventually fizzle out. This thought obsessed my mind for a full year. In all my spare moments of thought and all my quiet times I thought of this. I became angry and raged within myself on the absurdity of it all. I could not accept in my heart that when we die that was the end of existence--but I had no logical alternative. I had never been exposed to any other teaching. My life on the outside continued as normal but my life on the inside was turmoil. I could not understand how I could have a mind to question but be given no answers; this enraged me. I desperately needed an answer from this mental trap, when I had a dream.

In the dream I find myself sitting naked in the "thinker's position" with my chin on my fist. I am thinking the same thought that had plagued me for the entire previous year: "What happens when you die?" Suddenly I am addressed by a voice that seems to come from everywhere. The voice asks this question: "Do you want to know what it's like to die?"

This is a crazy question, I think to myself. Every cell in every part of my body then reacts. I look up and state with incredulity, "What do you think I've been asking for the last year?" I do not expect the answer that I receive. The voice says, "Okay—you're dead!"

Anxiously I think that I do not really want to die just to find out what happens when you eventually die, but before I can finish thinking the thought, I hear a loud crack of thunder and find myself traveling through an upwardly sloped tunnel with great speed. I travel for what seems to me to be about 15 seconds through more and more quickly passing arcs of light. I wonder if the light represents time.

The tunnel then ends and I find myself in a park sitting on a bench. There is a lake in front of me with trees and walking paths. Birds are singing their songs and there are other people in the park, walking along enjoying the scene. I even see a woman walking her baby through the park in a baby carriage. As I survey the scene I think to myself, "Hey, this isn't too bad..." and then instantly open my eyes to find myself in my bedroom of my own apartment.

I was so pleased with what I had experienced that I have never been seriously bothered by the thought of death since.

The "thinker's position" is the chin-on-hand pose of the naked seated man sculpted by Rodin. This famous sculpture has come to represent an archetypal image of serious thought about weighty matters. Interestingly, in dreams nudity is often a symbol of the "naked truth."

Later, Tom came across the writings of Robert Monroe, the out-of-body explorer who ventured into the transition places to the afterlife. In his first book, *Journeys Out of the Body*, Monroe described a scene he called "The Park." It is a post-death way station for incoming souls to relax, rest and meet with deceased friends and relatives, and with guides. On one of his out-of-body excursions, Monroe said:

> ...I ended up in a park-like surrounding, with carefully tended flowers, trees, and grass, much like a large mall with paths crisscrossing the area. There were benches along the paths, and there were hundreds of men and women strolling by, or sitting on the benches. Some were quite calm, others a little apprehensive, and many had a dazed or shocked look of disorientation. They appeared uncertain, unknowing of what to do or what was to take place next.
>
> Somehow I knew that this was a meeting place, where newly arrived waited for friends or relatives. From this Place of Meeting, these friends would take each newcomer to the proper place where he or she "belonged."

Many years later, Monroe returned to The Park in another excursion in his astral body, which he described in his last book prior to his death, *The Ultimate Journey*. While out searching for a dead friend, Monroe was reminded by a guide figure about The Park, and so goes there:

> It was the same as when I had visited many years ago, with winding walks, benches, flowers and shrubbery, different-colored grass lawns, clusters of stately trees, small streams and fountains, and with a warm sun overhead among small cumulus clouds. The Park continued on a gently rolling terrain as far as I could see.

Monroe realized something he could not have perceived years earlier from his more limited perspective: The Park is a place of human creation, made by human thought. He was soon met by a woman from one of his past lives. She said:

> I am only the messenger. I am to tell you that you may by all means bring people to us, those who are newly physically dead. We will take care of them. That is why we are here. And you may teach others to do this. ...It is a wholly objective way to remove the fear of physical death.

The woman explained that The Park was created by "a human civilization many thousands of years ago," and it does not cease to exist if a person does not believe in it. Souls come here to make a transition, she said; they are shown their many options for the afterlife, which also are self-created. The only rule is that no one impose his or her will upon another.

This afterlife created by human thought intersects with concepts in Eastern mysticism. The Bardo Thodol, the Tibetan Book of the Dead, teaches that both life and death are dreamlike, illusory reproductions of one's own thoughts. A deceased person experiences thought-form visions that conform, positively or negatively, to his or her religion, background, consciousness, karma, and so on. The objective of the Bardo Thodol is to awaken the dreamer to Reality, to seek liberation of all states of phenomena (heaven and hell alike) by the attainment of nirvana, a supramundane, transcendent state of being, that is beyond illusion.

According to Monroe, everyone, regardless of their beliefs, goes to The Park immediately after death as a transition way station, and from there to points beyond.

Park visions of the Dreaming Saint

A park setting was visited by St. John Bosco, a 19th-century Italian Catholic priest who kept a detailed diary of his lucid and out-of-body dreams. Many of his dream experiences were reinforced with religious imagery and lessons. Bosco founded the Society of St. Francis de Sales, known as the Salesians, an order to help orphaned and disadvantaged boys.

In 1876, Bosco had an intense lucid dream where he was taken to a park-like landscape:

> It seemed to me that I was standing on a hill, looking down on an immense plain that stretched away into the invisible distance. It was as blue as the sea in perfect calm, but what I was looking at was not water; it seemed like crystal, unblemished and sparkling.
>
> Long and broad avenues divided the plain up into large gardens of indescribable beauty, in which were lawns, groves or ornamental trees, flowering shrubs and flower-beds with an amazing variety of ornamental flowers. What you have seen in gardens can give you little idea of how wonderful all this was. There were trees whose leaves seemed to be of gold, the branches and trunks of precious stones.
>
> Scattered here and there in the gardens were buildings whose appearance and magnificence rivaled the setting in which they stood. I could not estimate what immense sums of money even one of these would have cost to build. The thought ran through my head: "If I could have any one of these buildings for my boys, how happy they would be."
>
> As I stood there rapt in wonder, the sound of sweet and entrancing

music filled the air; all possible instruments seemed to be combining in wonderful harmony, and together with them choirs of singers.

I then saw great numbers of people in the garden, some walking, some sitting, all radiantly happy. Some were singing, some playing instruments, and it was obvious that they derived equal pleasure from hearing the others as they did from the music they were making themselves. They were singing in Latin these words: "All honor and glory to God the Almighty Father—Creator of the ages, who was, who is and who will come to judge the living and the dead through all ages."

The park-like setting was lit by an intense, brilliant light. Bosco was met by Dominic Salvo, one of his young charges who had died at age 15. Bosco asked him:

> "Where am I?" I asked.
>
> "You are in a place of happiness," he replied, "where all that is beautiful can be enjoyed."
>
> "Is this Heaven, then?"
>
> "No, whatever is here is of the earth, although improved beyond conception by the power of God. No living person can ever see or imagine the wonders of eternity."
>
> "Would it be possible to have natural light more brilliant than this?"
>
> "Yes, quite possible ... look there in the distance."
>
> I looked, and a ray of light suddenly appeared, so penetrating and of such brilliance that I had to close my eyes, and I cried out in alarm so loudly that I woke the priest who was sleeping in the room nearby. I opened my eyes after a moment and said: "But that is surely a ray of the divine light ..."
>
> "No, even that does not give you any idea. In heaven we enjoy God, and that is everything."

Here, too, is reinforcement that after death, souls enjoy a place of transition that is one of great beauty and light. The splendor of a garden or park is known to everyone and evokes a universal response of peace and pleasure.

A beautiful field where children can play

Park-like settings have been described in dreams and visions about children who die. Susan C. is an experienced hospice nurse who works with terminally ill children. Some of her young charges have suffered from spinal muscle atrophy, a condition in which muscles gradually deteriorate until the child is paralyzed, and suffocates. The last thing to go before death are the facial muscles, making these cases particularly tragic. The little bodies lie still and limp, but the minds are alert and the faces can smile.

After working with the children for a while, Susan told me that she began experiencing unusual dreams with several of her terminally ill children. The dreams were full of brilliant imagery and intense joy and happiness, and they occurred just before—or just as—a child died. At first Susan felt guilty about these dreams, which seem so enjoyable—until she understood what was happening.

One of Susan's cases was a seven-month-old boy, Z., who suffered from spinal muscle atrophy. The condition was discovered when, at age three to four months, he came down with pneumonia. He was taken to the hospital but did not get better. More tests were done, and the disease was discovered. His parents were devastated, and wanted to do whatever they could to prolong and save his life. He was fitted with a respiratory device that went through the mouth and nose, and his parents took him home.

Little Z. deteriorated as the disease took its toll. He had to be on constant life support. Heartbroken at watching their baby suffer, the parents at last made the agonizing decision to turn off his life support system. Susan was informed and went to their home. The life support was disconnected, but Z. was able to breathe on his own through the night. By 6 AM he was still alive, and the mother told Susan to lie down and get some rest. When she did, Susan was transported to another world:

> I had the most magnificent dream. It was a beautiful field with chil-
> dren all around. We were playing, riding horses and petting them, and
> roaming in the field. Animals were everywhere. It was incredibly beautiful,
> beautiful. While I was dreaming the mother came and woke me up. I was
> disoriented. She told me Z. was gone. I had this tremendous guilt that here
> I was, having this dream while the baby was passing away, and I wasn't
> there for support like I should have been.

Susan remained disturbed by this experience. She was supposed to be one of the best in her field—how could she be having fun in a dream when she should have been alert?

About a year later, she was caring for another baby boy, W., who suffered from the same disease. She was also pregnant with her own baby. She constantly dreamed of W. walking and climbing around, even though he could not do those things in waking life. The parents tried many measures to help their child, including faith healing. Nothing worked.

One night, when Susan was five months along, she fell into an exhausted, deep sleep at home.

> I had an incredible dream with W. flying around, playing and run-
> ning. He lasted two more months. The night he died, I had that same
> dream about the beautiful field and the children playing. The phone rang
> and woke me up. I just knew he was gone.

Another child, a girl suffering from spinal muscle atrophy, was under Susan's care on and off for more than seven years while the child lived in an iron lung. She had been in the iron lung since nine months of age. Up until she was about two to three, she could be taken out for an hour or two at a time, but then the ravages of the disease required her to be in the lung around the clock.

When the little girl was seven years old, shortly before she died, Susan began having vivid dreams of her calling to Susan, asking her to play.

In these dreams the children are always playing with me. The disheartening thing is that the children I take care of can't play. They just lay flaccid. You might get a little arm movement. The only thing they can do is smile and laugh.

In the dreams there are butterflies and horses, and always a field with flowers and trees. It's always the most beautiful, peaceful dream I've ever had. Each time there are different children there, and we play different games. We play ring around the rosie a lot, and I can feel the touching hands. I can feel the ponies when we pet them. The dreams feel very real to me. I wake up with my heart is accelerating and feel like I was actually running and playing and touching them.

In addition to the dreams that preceded or accompanied the death of a child, Susan always felt anxiety after awakening. Then she realized that perhaps the dreams were the only way her paralyzed children could reach out to her and say good-bye. In the dreamscape we are freed from the bonds of the body.

I now see the dreams as very liberating. You want the children to have joy and comfort. Their brains are working but their bodies aren't. You try to think of ways to play with them. Playing in the dreams gave me a lot of joy. The children were always telling me not to be sad. I was always teary-eyed in the dreams, but it was a full-of-joy-teary-eyed.

I'm not certain the field is heaven, but I do feel that heaven is a place of great joy and beauty. I've been able to release the guilt I felt. These dreams have helped me to redefine my purpose through God or the universe, and not through my ego, wanting to be the best.

The dream state provided a place where souls in their second bodies could meet and experience the gift of love and joy.

A beautiful farewell

Beautiful scenes of an afterlife appear in farewell dreams and visions. In *Parting Visions*, Melvin Morse told of a woman who had a dream or vision of her baby at the moment the infant died of SIDS (Sudden Infant Death Syndrome). "Linda" was in her twenties, and had put her baby down for a nap in her crib. She had no inkling of anything wrong. Tired herself, Linda lay down for a nap and went to sleep. She said:

> All of a sudden it was like I was there. I could see a beautiful country that seemed to be made of light. The hills and the grass were spectacular. There were various shades of light that glowed in the most generous way.
>
> I could see my daughter there in this field, a place that looked like a meadow. She wasn't lying there, but she wasn't walking, either. Maybe she was floating.
>
> I felt as though I had finally come home, as though this "beyond" place was where I should be. And then I woke up.

Linda awakened with a start and instinctively knew the baby was in trouble. She ran to the crib—but the child had already died. Later, during her grieving, Linda found the dream to be comforting, because she had glimpsed where her child was going.

The other side of the river

As a child, dream researcher Val Bigelow had a recurring dream about the "other side" of a river, which she later saw as a glimpse of the Other Side or the afterlife:

> In real life, our family lived in nice apartment building in the very northernmost section of the Bronx. About two or three blocks to the west

of where we lived was the Bronx River, a north-south flowing river with a nice, well-used green park all along its banks. I only recently realized that on the other or western bank, of the Bronx River was the huge Woodlawn Cemetery, well treed, fenced and with many elaborate statues.

The dream always started with me on our side of the Bronx River somehow swimming, wading or getting across it to the other side. The feeling of the other side was always happy, fun, joyful, even numinous. I would often seem to spend a lot of time over there with many friends (friends I didn't know in my six-, seven-, or eight-year-old life here). I got the impression that these friends were more adult than my chronological age, and maybe I was, too.

Toward the end of the dream I had to make my way back across to "my" side of the river and when I did this I would wake up. I would be sorry to wake from that dream and hope I would have it again.

It is only now, as an adult and dream researcher, that I believe that those dreams may have been real excursions to the Other Side, and only today that I realize the added symbolism of the cemetery being on the other side of the river too (although in the dream state there wasn't a cemetery there, but a wonderful place with a feeling like a fair or happy amusement park). I wonder how many other children may have had similar dream experiences with the other side?

An interesting touch of archetypal symbolism in Val's dreams is that the Other Side is across a river and is to the west. In many mythologies around the world, the dead must cross a river or other body of water in order to reach the land of the dead. In Greek mythology, the River Styx separates the world of the living from Hades, the Underworld. The dead are ferried across in a boat by Charon. (It remained a custom throughout Europe well into later centuries to bury the dead with coins placed on the eyes to pay for the ferryman.) The west, the direction of the setting sun, has long been associated with the Underworld. The ancient Egyptians buried their kings, queen and nobility on the western bank of the Nile at Thebes (now Luxor). West was the direction of the Hall of Amenti, the realm of the dead.

According to The Book of the Dead (which the Egyptians called The Book of Coming Forth By Day), souls of the dead had to navigate treacherous swamp-like areas and waters in their underworld journey.

Traditionally, the land of the dead cannot be accessed easily by the living. This is reinforced in NDEs, in which experiencers reach a point of no return, such as a bridge or an entrance to a garden. They know, or are told by a guide figure or voice, that if they cross the threshold they cannot go back to life but will be irrevocably in the land of the dead. Some are told by their guides that they must go back because they have not completed what they are supposed to do in life, while others are given a choice.

Mediums who contact the dead also speak of a one-way barrier. The dead seem to be able to meet the living under certain circumstances and for a limited time, such as through mediumship or dreams, but we cannot attempt go to them in their realm without great peril.

Going to heaven to find God

Myrtle Fillmore, the co-founder of the Unity School of Nondenominational Christianity, believed strongly in dreams for spiritual guidance, as did her husband, Charles. The couple founded Unity in 1889 after both of them had experienced miraculous healing through prayer. Charles had a lame leg from a skating accident, and Myrtle became seriously ill with tuberculosis.

Following her recovery from tuberculosis, Myrtle enjoyed a long life of robust energy. She did have bouts of sickness, however, as we all do. She believed that if she maintained the right state of consciousness, the healing power of God would keep flowing through her. Once when Myrtle was not feeling well, she had a dream that reminded her where to find the true healing power of God:

For some days I had not been my usual self, and finally I had to go to bed. The world would say I was sick, dangerously ill, but I knew better. The trouble was that I had allowed some thought of negation to creep into my consciousness, and that thought was inhibiting the free flow of God's perfect health in my body. I knew that just as soon as I replaced that negative thought with the realization of "God is my health, I can't be sick," I should be well. With this thought on my lips I went to sleep.

Myrtle then had a dream in which she found herself in heaven, where she conversed with an angel:

The sky was so blue and the fields were so green, and the flowers everywhere—I can't tell you how beautiful it was—just like a dream! As I walked down the road, I met a beautiful woman dressed in a pure white robe with a gold girdle. She had wonderful golden hair and she smiled at me sweetly and said, "How are you this fine day?"

"Very well," I faltered, "but can you tell me where I am?"

"Why, don't you know? You're in heaven."

I looked around in amazement. Then I looked at the woman, but I couldn't say a word. Then I thought of how as a little girl I had tried to imagine what heaven was like. I turned to the woman again and faltered, "Are you an angel?"

"Yes," she smiled, "I'm an angel. Wouldn't you like to be one too?"

"I suppose so," I replied, "but where's God? I'd like to see him."

"God! Why do you wish to see him?"

Her question puzzled me. Why wouldn't anyone want to see God!

Still perplexed I replied, "That's one reason why I wanted to come to heaven—to see Him."

"Did you think that you had to come to heaven to find Him?"

"Well—I thought that I should find him here. I was looking for Him when I met you, although I wasn't sure this was heaven."

"Where did you look?"

"Oh, I looked all about me! I thought that perhaps this road would take me to his palace."

"Dear one," the angel said in a tone full of assurance. "He has no palace. He is all about you. He is here. He is with you now as He was on earth. But you will not find Him unless you look within yourself. At the center of your being He abides forever. Turn within and know that God is here."

Myrtle awakened abruptly, charged with emotion. The "dream" had seemed so real that at first she was not sure where she was:

I looked about me. Where was I? Why—I was in my own bed; but something was changed. Through my mind rang the words, "God is here. God is here." I sat up exclaiming, "Yes, God is here, and in His presence I am well." I got up and dressed. When a friend came in a few moments later she found me as well and strong as ever.

Swedenborg's afterlife dream visions

The mystical dreams and visions of Emanuel Swedenborg support the idea of a self-created afterlife. Swedenborg, born in 1688, was a scientist and scholar who gave little thought to spiritual matters until he experienced a breakthrough of ecstatic visions in 1743 at age 56. Up to that time he had not given much thought to spiritual matters, although he believed in the existence of the soul. Suddenly he was overcome with revelations about heaven and hell, the work of angels and spirits, the true meaning of Scripture and the order of the universe.

Swedenborg's experiences demonstrate the overlap between dreams, waking visions, out-of-body travel to other dimensions, and near-death experiences. He could enter dream-like trance states for up to three days. During these times, his breathing would be severely reduced and he would be insensible, but his mental activity remained sharp. He maintained that he was fully conscious during the visions. He once likened his trances to what happens when a person dies and is resuscitated—what is now called the NDE.

Swedenborg also had an unusual ability to remain for prolonged periods in the borderland state between sleep and wakefulness, either as he was going to sleep or as he was awakening. In this twilight state of entwined wakefulness and dreaming, one is immersed in vivid images and voices. It is possible to have sustained interactions that are more difficult in different dream states. Swedenborg called his visionary travels being "in the spirit," and he clearly knew that he was out of his body. He believed that angels cause our dreams, and that dream imagery corresponds to the thoughts and feelings of angels.

In 1744 and 1745, Swedenborg had visions that had a profound effect on him, and greatly opened his spiritual senses. He later said he was able to exist simultaneously in the material world and the spiritual realms. He was convinced that God had selected him to be his spiritual emissary, and quit his post as assessor in 1747 at age 59 to devote himself to his visionary work for the remainder of his life; he died in 1772.

Swedenborg said that God created humans to exist simultaneously in the physical and spiritual worlds. The spiritual world is an inner domain that influences humankind, though most persons have lost their awareness of it. The inner world survives death with its own eternal memory of every thought, emotion and action accumulated over a lifetime. The memory thus influences the soul's fate of heaven or hell.

After death, souls enter an earth-like transition plane called "The Spirit World" where they are met by dead relatives and friends. After a period of self-evaluation, they choose their heaven or hell. The afterworlds are products of the mind created during life on earth. (Swedenborg did not believe that Jesus's crucifixion automatically absolved the sins of humankind.) Hell is frightening and desolate, with souls with monstrous faces, but has no Satan by Christian definition. Heaven is a replication of earth; human souls become "angels." In both spheres, souls carry on life in physical-like bodies and pursue work, leisure, and marriage. In hell, war and crime prevail, and excesses of vice and evil are punished. Both spheres have societal structures and governments. According to Swedenborg, it is possible for souls to advance in the afterlife, but never to leave heaven or hell, which are permanent states. He did not believe in reincarnation.

However, heaven and hell are not all there is to the afterlife. Swedenborg said that beyond heaven is another heaven, made up of a brilliant streaming of light.

Swedenborg was actively opposed by the Christian church. His ideas were popular in the 19th century among Transcendentalists, artists and philosophers. Spiritualists, who adopted many of Swedenborg's views, refer to the afterlife as "Summerland," which evokes a park-like imagery. Of his various books, Heaven and Hell offers the most detail about the afterlife.

Dreams of hell

Dreams about a hellish or unpleasant afterlife occur to many people, but usually with a different context than previewing the afterlife. Hell dreams often represent issues involving guilt and fear of punishment for mistakes and transgressions, and concern daily life.

What dreams tell us about the Other Side

Dreams offer us reassurance of continuing life in another realm that is permeated with beauty, peace and happiness. The afterlife presented in dreams indicates that earthly suffering is ended, redemption is possible, and states of being are fluid and changeable.

13

Dream Sending to the Afterlife

Encounters with the dead in dreams help us through grief and unfinished business, and stressful times in daily life. They open the door to the Other Side, convincing us or confirming for us survival after death. The give us a glimpse of eternity, and raise our bond with other souls to a new level of consciousness.

As we've seen throughout the book, the conditions by which afterlife dreams are generated are quite variable. Emotional bonds are an important factor. The recipient of afterlife dreams either has a strong connection to the dead, or to another person related to the dead. Psychic sensitivity may heighten the ability to receive afterlife dreams, but afterlife dreams are not dependent on that faculty.

Sometimes afterlife dreams do not happen, no matter how much a person wants and prays for one. It may be that dreams are the not best medium for contact for certain individuals, depending on unknown conditions on both side of the veil. Most likely, some other form of contact has already occurred, and may even have been overlooked. Signs and synchroniticies also are common ways for the dead to reach out to the living.

Out-of-body awareness

Learning how to recognize out-of-body states in dreaming may enhance a person's ability to have extraordinary dreams. Robert Monroe discovered that if he tried to retain conscious awareness as he drifted into sleep, he entered a state he called "mind awake body asleep."

To follow Monroe's procedure, relax the body and allow yourself to begin to drift down. When in the twilight state of hypnagogic sleep, similar to dozing in which you still retain conscious awareness, think about becoming lighter and lighter, until you rise up and move away. Monroe called this "lift-off," and said it is the easiest way to separate from the physical body. You may have a sensation of going out through the top of your head, or suddenly being in your subtle or astral body.

Monroe also used a technique which he called "rotation" or "peel-off." While lying prone on your back and in the hypnagogic state, slowly turn over without using your arms or legs for assistance. When you have turned 180 degrees, think of floating up and away, as though backing up from the body.

A dream sending exercise

One way to invite an afterlife dream is to send a dream to the afterlife. Dreams have telepathic potential, as demonstrated in the ability of dreams to perceive future events, and in all types of afterlife dreams, in which communication is telepathic in nature. Sigmund Freud observed that "sleep creates favorable conditions for telepathy," and referred often to dream telepathy in his clinical work with patients. Dream telepathy has been validated in scientific studies, such as at the dream laboratory at Maimonides Medical Center in Brooklyn. During the 1960s, dramatic dream telepathy experiments were documented by researchers Montague Ullman, Stanley Krippner and psychic Alan Vaughan.

Dream sending is based on ancient practices that take advantage of the natural telepathic capabilities of dreams. The ancients, knowing that gods and spiritual figures visited people in dreams and conveyed messages, did rituals for sending dreams in order to influence the thoughts and actions of others. Sometimes sent dreams were intended to appear as instructions from the gods.

Dream sending is an invitation for the door between worlds to open. It does not guarantee an afterlife dream, but it does focus attention on dreams, and sharpens our dreamwork skills. The technique is simple:

1. Compose a message.

Keep the message short, in bold and vivid words that carry a lot of emotion. Whether it is a statement, request or a question, the emotional tone is important in the ability of consciousness to travel across the bridge. It may be helpful to concentrate on the message for a day or more. Hold it within the heart.

2. Build a mental picture of the recipient.

Like the message, make your mental picture as bold and vivid as possible. Put emotion into it. Dreams speak primarily in symbols and images, and an emotionally charged image, such as two people reuniting, adds a great deal of energy. Visualize the dead as you remember them best. You may have an impression of how they are in their new state, but if not, do not be concerned about being "right"—your emotional connection is what matters the most. If the recipient is a spiritual being or guide, let your imagination guide you in building a mental image. Trust your intuition.

3. Build a mental picture of where you can connect.

Afterlife dream meetings often take place at home in familiar surroundings, or in a location between worlds. Try visualizing a doorway, a bridge, a park, or even a seamless white environment lit with pleasant golden-white light.

4. Prior to sleep, program your dreams with your intention.

Hold the intention to connect as you fall asleep, along with the instruction to yourself that you will recall all the details of your dream when you awaken.

5. Upon awakening, write down everything that you can remember.

Record even the smallest details, even if nothing seems to fit your objective. You may have an "ordinary" dream instead of a lucid visitation dream, but ordinary dreams also contain valuable information. It is helpful to learn some basics of dream symbol interpretation; try my *Pocket Dream Guide and Dictionary.*

6. Stay alert for messages coming in other ways.

Dream sending may be answered via different channels, such as waking visions, mental impressions, synchronicity, other dreams later, and so on.

Knowing when to let go

While it is helpful and healing to have reassuring contact with the dead, it is not a good idea to try to prolong contact. Once on the Other Side, the dead continue with their own existence and evolution, moving into different regions. To constantly pull them back into our dreams and lives hinders both the living and the dead from advancing and growing. It prevents us from fully accepting their death, and inhibits their own activity. In dreams and in messages channeled through mediums, the dead stress that they want to reassure loved ones they are all right, but they also stress that it is important not to hold on to them through grief or through constant contact efforts.

This does not mean we should not honor the dead, think of them, or hold them in loving thoughts and prayers. These are all important acts that send out streams of high level spiritual energy. There is a difference when it comes to holding on and holding down. Deep in your heart you know when that line is crossed.

The dead have much to share, and we have much to learn, about dying and the afterlife. Our afterlife dreams play an important role in the growth of our consciousness.

About the Author

Rosemary Ellen Guiley is a leading expert in the paranormal, metaphysical, and spiritual fields, and is the author of more than 50 books, including the *Pocket Dream Guide and Dictionary* and five other books on dreams. She has been a lay facilitator of dreamwork since the early 1990s, helping people explore their dreams in one-on-one and group settings. She also conducts workshops on developing intuitive and psychic ability. She is a former board member of the International Association for the Study of Dreams. Rosemary is a frequent guest on *Coast to Coast AM* where she often discusses dreams. Her website is www.visionaryliving.com.

Bibliography

Barrett, William. *Death-Bed Visions: The Psychical Experiences of the Dying.* Wellingborough, Northhamptonshire: The Aquarian Press, 1986.

Berger, Arthur S. *Evidence of Life After Death: A Casebook for the Tough-Minded.* Springfield, IL: Charles C Thomas, 1988.

Bulkeley, Kelly. *Spiritual Dreaming: A Cross-Cultural and Historical Journey.* New York/Mahwah, N.J. Paulist Press, 1995.

Callanan, Maggie and Patricia Kelley. *Final Gifts: Understanding the Special Awareness, Needs, and Communications of the Dying.* New York: Simon & Schuster, 2012.

"Case of the Will of James L. Chaffin." *Proceedings of the Society for Psychical Research*, 1928, 36, 103:517-524.

Guiley, Rosemary Ellen. *The Dreamer's Way.* New York: Berkley Books, 2004.

_____. *Dreamspeak: How to Understand the Messages in Your Dreams.* New York: Berkley Books, 2001.

_____. *Dreamwork for the Soul.* New York: Berkley Books, 1998.

Gurney, Edmund, and Frederic W.H. Myers and Frank Podmore. *Phantasms of the Living.* London: Kegan Paul, Trench, Trubner & Co. Ltd., 1918.

Heath, Pamela Rae and Jon Klimo. *Suicide: What Really Happens in the Afterlife? Channeled Conversations with the Dead*. Berkeley, CA: North Atlantic Books, 2006.

Kubler-Ross, Elisabeth. *On Death and Dying*. New York: Scribner, 1997.

Martin, Joel and Patricia Romanowski. *Love Beyond Life: The Healing Power of After-Death Communications*. New York: HarperCollins Publishers, 1997.

McEneaney, Bonnie. *Messages: Signs, Visits and Premonitions from Loved Ones Lost on 9/11*. New York: William Morrow/HarperCollins, 2010.

Morse, Melvin with Paul Perry. Parting Visions: *Uses and Meanings of Pre-Death, Psychic, and Spiritual Experiences*. New York: Villard Books, 1994.

Myers, Frederic W.H. *Human Personality and Its Survival of Bodily Death Vols. I & II*. New York: Longmans, Green & Co., 1954.

Noory, George and Rosemary Ellen Guiley. *Talking to the Dead*. New York: Tor Books, 2011.

Osis, Karlis. *Deathbed Observations by Physicians and Nurses*. Monograph No. 3. New York: Parapsychology Foundation, 1961.

Osis, Karlis and Erlendur Haraldsson. *At the Hour of Death*. New York: Hastings House, 1986.

Ring, Kenneth. *Lessons from the Light: What We Can Learn About the Near-Death Experience*. Needham, MA: Moment Point Press, 1988.

_____. *Heading Toward Omega: In Search of the Meaning of the Near-Death Experience.* New York: William Morrow, 1984.

Sanford, John A. *Dreams: God's Forgotten Language.* San Francisco: Harper & Row, 1968.

Sheldrake, Rupert. *Dogs That Know When Their Owners Are Coming Home: Fully Updated and Revised.* New York: Broadway Books, 2011.

Sheridan, Kim. *Animals and the Afterlife: True Stories of Our Best Friends' Journey Beyond Death.* Carlsbad, CA: Hay House, 2006.

Von Franz, Marie Louise. *On Dreams and Death.* Boston: Shambhala Publications, 1984.

Wills-Brandon, Carla. *One Last Hug Before I Go: The Mystery and Meaning of Deathbed Visions.* Deerfield Beach, FL: HCI, 2000.